TExES

English Language Arts and Reading 7-12 Practice Questions

TExES Practice Tests & Exam Review for the Texas Examinations of Educator Standards

Mometrix
TEST PREPARATION

Dear Future Exam Success Story

First of all, **THANK YOU** for purchasing Mometrix study materials!

Second, congratulations! You are one of the few determined test-takers who are committed to doing whatever it takes to excel on your exam. **You have come to the right place.** We developed these practice tests with one goal in mind: to deliver you the best possible approximation of the questions you will see on test day.

Standardized testing is one of the biggest obstacles on your road to success, which only increases the importance of doing well in the high-pressure, high-stakes environment of test day. Your results on this test could have a significant impact on your future, and these practice tests will give you the repetitions you need to build your familiarity and confidence with the test content and format to help you achieve your full potential on test day.

Your success is our success

We would love to hear from you! If you would like to share the story of your exam success or if you have any questions or comments in regard to our products, please contact us at **800-673-8175** or **support@mometrix.com**.

Thanks again for your business and we wish you continued success!

Sincerely,
The Mometrix Test Preparation Team

TABLE OF CONTENTS

Practice Test #1

1. Among digital networking's educational advantages, which most transforms social interactions?

a. Linking digitally saved resources to one another
b. Embedded links to references and learning supports
c. Virtually instant access to global communications
d. Diverse formats more similar to diverse learners

2. Regarding the standard conventions for written English when evaluating student writing, which of the following reflects the function of writing rather than its form?

a. The length of the student's composition
b. Appropriate content in the composition
c. Word usage in a student's composition
d. The spelling in a student's composition

3. Which of the following would be most useful in assessing and documenting students' language progress throughout a school year?

a. An audio/video recording of each student reading the same text at the beginning of the year and again at the end of the year
b. A portfolio including pre-tests, post-tests, vocabulary work, journal entries, writing assignments, group projects, and other relevant work from throughout the year
c. Score composites and details from state- and national-referenced exams or other standardized tests.
d. A detailed narrative composed by the student's teacher, detailing strengths, weaknesses, and descriptions of the student's work.

4. Arthur writes a paper. One classmate identifies ideas and words that resonated with her when she read it. Another describes how reading the paper changed his thinking. A third asks Arthur some questions about what he meant by certain statements in the paper. A fourth suggests that a portion of the paper needs more supporting information. Which of the following is taking place?

a. A portfolio assessment
b. A writing workshop
c. A holistic scoring
d. A peer review

5. Which of the following strategies is most effective in encouraging reluctant families to participate in the education program?

a. Communicating through a variety of means, such as phone calls, emails, and handwritten notes
b. Providing multiple opportunities for involvement, such as inviting families to visit the classroom, hosting open-house nights, scheduling conferences, and requesting volunteers
c. Seeking professional development opportunities focused on culturally competent communication strategies
d. Posting important updates and information about curriculum on a class website

6. Which of the following examples best describes explicit and systematic phonics instruction?

a. A teacher observes a student as he reads a book independently. When the student struggles to decode a word with a certain spelling pattern, the teacher intervenes and provides a mini-lesson on the skill.
b. A teacher assesses her students' phonics skills regularly and uses the assessment data to plan flexible, targeted, small-group instruction on specific sounds and blends.
c. A teacher conducts frequent surveys to learn more about her students' interests. She uses the results to select books on these topics. She then identifies a few phonics skills that can be taught using the text in each book.
d. A teacher reads a big book aloud to her students. She stops on a page and asks students if they notice any patterns in the words. Students identify words that start with the same letter, end with the same suffixes, and more. The teacher briefly explains each of their observations.

7. When asking a research question, which of the following should a researcher do first?

a. Search the literature for knowledge gaps related to the topic
b. Search the literature for definitive answers to that question
c. Search the literature for additional research needs or openings
d. Search the literature for consensus or controversy on the topic

8. What most accurately identifies the kind(s) of opportunities teachers are expected to give students with respect to literature?

a. To read different literary genres independently only
b. To hear literature read aloud in addition to reading it
c. To respond to literature by writing and speaking on it
d. To read, listen, and respond to literature and to interact with other students

9. Which mode of writing is most suitable for the purpose of encouraging the reading audience to explore ideas and consider various potential associated responses?

a. Narrative
b. Expository
c. Persuasive
d. Speculative

10. Which of these is NOT a benefit of a well-organized essay?

a. A well-organized essay is more likely to gain readers' acceptance of its thesis as valid.
b. A well-organized essay is more likely to hold readers' attention.
c. A well-organized essay requires less effort to write but more effort to read and understand.
d. A well-organized essay makes it easier for readers to identify the main ideas and the evidence that supports them.

11. As a reading strategy, ELA teachers can best give students practice in making predictions to support comprehension through which activity?

a. Predicting what or whom a book is about
b. Predicting what a novel's character will do
c. Predicting a significant event in a narrative
d. Predicting (B) and/or (C), rather than (A)

12. At the beginning of each month, Mr. Yi has Jade read a page or two from a book she hasn't seen before. He notes the total number of words in the section and the number of times she leaves out or misreads a word. If Jade reads the passage with less than 3% error, Mr. Yi is satisfied that Jade is:

a. Reading with full comprehension
b. Probably bored and should try a more difficult book
c. Reading at her independent reading level
d. Comfortable with the syntactical meaning

13. Authors of technical informational text may need to write in nontechnical language for which of the following reasons?

a. To communicate denser content rather than clear messages
b. To inform other professionals working in relevant fields
c. To present effective proposals that secure funding for projects to people or organizations who may or may not be familiar with the subject matter
d. To explain concepts to a select few experts

14. Which of the following is an example of a summative assessment?

a. Final project critiques
b. Oral question-and-answer sessions
c. Running records
d. Pop quizzes

Refer to the following for question 15:

It is a truth universally acknowledged, that a single man in possession of a good fortune, must be in want of a wife.

However little known the feelings or views of such a man may be on his first entering a neighbourhood, this truth is so well fixed in the minds of the surrounding families, that he is considered the rightful property of some one or other of their daughters.

"My dear Mr. Bennet," said his lady to him one day, "have you heard that Netherfield Park is let at last?"

Mr. Bennet replied that he had not.

"But it is," returned she; "for Mrs. Long has just been here, and she told me all about it."

Mr. Bennet made no answer.

"Do you not want to know who has taken it?" cried his wife impatiently.

"You want to tell me, and I have no objection to hearing it."

This was invitation enough.

"Why, my dear, you must know, Mrs. Long says that Netherfield is taken by a young man of large fortune from the north of England; that he came down on Monday in a chaise and four to see the place, and was so much delighted with it, that he agreed with Mr. Morris immediately; that he is to take possession before Michaelmas, and some of his servants are to be in the house by the end of next week."

"What is his name?"

"Bingley."

"Is he married or single?"

"Oh! Single, my dear, to be sure! A single man of large fortune; four or five thousand a year. What a fine thing for our girls!"

"How so? How can it affect them?"

"My dear Mr. Bennet," replied his wife, "how can you be so tiresome! You must know that I am thinking of his marrying one of them."

"Is that his design in settling here?"

"Design! Nonsense, how can you talk so! But it is very likely that he may fall in love with one of them, and therefore you must visit him as soon as he comes."

"I see no occasion for that. You and the girls may go, or you may send them by themselves, which perhaps will be still better, for as you are as handsome as any of them, Mr. Bingley may like you the best of the party."

[Adapted from Jane Austen, *Pride and Prejudice* (1813)]

15. This selection is set in England at the beginning of the 19th century. Drawing on information from this selection, what could you conclude was a primary goal for young women in England during this time period?

a. To marry a man who wants a wife
b. To marry a man with money
c. To entertain the neighbors
d. To find and attract wealthy neighbors to move nearby

16. Some experts maintain that teaching reading comprehension entails not only the application of skills but also the process of actively constructing meaning. They describe this process as interactive, strategic, and adaptable. Which of the following descriptions best applies to the interactive aspect of this process?

a. The process involves the text, the reader, and the context in which reading occurs.
b. The process involves readers using a variety of strategies in constructing meaning.
c. The process involves readers changing their strategies to read different text types.
d. The process involves changing strategies according to different reasons for reading.

17. Which of the following statements most accurately compares the components of speeches and the components of essays?

a. Speeches and essays have similar introductions.
b. Speeches provide supporting evidence in greater detail than essays do.
c. The conclusion of a speech must be more forceful and engaging than the conclusion of an essay.
d. Speeches may include greetings, mentions of honored guests, and thanks, but essays should not include these elements.

18. A teacher asks students to close their eyes while she reads a descriptive, fictional text aloud. When she is done reading, students draw pictures of the story's setting and share their pictures with the class. Which reading strategy are students practicing?

a. Predicting
b. Inferring
c. Summarizing
d. Visualizing

19. What is correct about evidence-based instructional strategies to use with ELL students?

a. Asking ELL students to explain and/or retell what teachers said to classmates is useful.
b. To get ELLs to concentrate on language, teachers should avoid incorporating visual aids.
c. Teachers should not "talk down" to ELLs by presenting abstract ideas in concrete forms.
d. Teachers may have ELLs signal when they don't understand, but they should not elaborate verbally.

20. Following instruction time, Ms. Pitman provides each student with a small sign that can be hung around the waist or neck. Ten children in her class receive signs displaying a single weekly vocabulary word. Five students get signs with the following: *dis-*, *re-*, *pre-*, *un-*, and *mis-*. The remaining students have signs with the following: *-ing*, *-ed*, *-s*, *-less*, and *-ful*. What is the best choice for a follow-up class activity based on this information?

a. The students are arranged into groups to demonstrate tangibly that certain parts of the English language have fixed functions.
b. Each student must use his or her sign to brainstorm a list of possible words that include those letters.
c. Each time a bell is rung, students must find a new partner with whom he or she can combine signs to make a new word.
d. Ask each student to explain what his or her sign means and how it functions in the English language.

21. Which of the following students may need extra instruction and evaluation with respect to oral language skills?

a. Rosa: whose first language is Spanish. Rosa speaks with a distinct accent and can be difficult to understand when speaking about a new or unfamiliar topic.
b. Greer: who avoids oral assignments when possible. He avoids speaking up in class and only responds when called upon.
c. Ashley: who often has trouble answering questions in class. Her responses are often off-topic. She also struggles with oral presentations, seeming to present a string of unrelated facts.
d. Brett: who frequently becomes loud and disruptive whenever group work is assigned. He often becomes involved in heated discussions with classmates when discussing ideas.

22. Among persuasive methods of appeal, which of the following is NOT a writing technique that supports the author's views by quoting others who agree with them?

a. Anticipating objections
b. Citing expert opinions
c. Bandwagon appeals
d. Testimonials

23. Suppose a written or spoken argument's claim is that community colleges in your state have recently had their budgets cut. Which of these would be sufficient evidence to prove this claim?

a. Citing the largest budget cut at one college
b. Citing two prominent examples of the cuts
c. Citing examples from 15 of the 34 community colleges in the state
d. Citing specific cut amounts at all 34 colleges

24. To help students decode words of increasing complexity, a teacher instructs them in strategies, including identifying Greek and Latin roots, prefixes, and suffixes to establish meaning. Which of the following does this strategy exemplify?

a. Alphabetic principle knowledge
b. Combinations of vowel sounds
c. Semantic and syntactic context
d. Structural cues in morphology

Refer to the following for question 25:

The Nigerian Letter Fraud

Nigerian letter frauds are variations of advance fee schemes in which a letter, mailed from Nigeria, offers the recipient the "opportunity" to share in millions of dollars that the author, a self-proclaimed government official, is trying to transfer illegally out of Nigeria. The victim receives a letter or email asking him to send personal information: blank letterhead stationery, bank name and account numbers and other identifying information. Eventually, the scheme attempts to get the willing victim, who has demonstrated a propensity for larceny by responding to the invitation, to send money to the author of the letter in Nigeria in several installments of increasing amounts for a variety of reasons. Payment of taxes, bribes to government officials, and legal fees are often described in great detail with the promise that all expenses will be reimbursed as soon as the funds are spirited out of Nigeria. In reality, the millions of dollars do not exist and the victim gets nothing. In fact, once the victim stops sending money, the perpetrators have been known to use the personal information that they received to impersonate the victim, draining bank accounts and credit card balances. While such an invitation strikes most of us as a laughable hoax, millions of dollars in losses are caused by these schemes annually.

25. This paragraph is best described as which of the following?

a. Factual reporting
b. Humor
c. Fiction
d. Poetry

26. What is correct about how teachers can use rubrics as a research-based assessment method?

a. Teachers should use rubrics to conduct formative (not summative) student work assessments.
b. Teachers should use rubrics for lesson objectives, both to guide and to assess students' work.
c. Teachers should use rubrics to conduct summative (not formative) student work assessments.
d. Teachers should use rubrics in place of stating learning objectives and modeling performance.

27. When summarizing text as part of a comprehension strategy, which of the following is an attribute of a good summary?

a. A summary should be detailed.
b. A summary should be thorough.
c. A summary should mostly consist of main ideas.
d. A summary should repeat the information in a passage.

28. Which of the following is critically effective for the purposes and audiences of blog writing?

a. Writing with correct punctuation
b. Writing with longer paragraphs
c. Writing with longer sentences
d. Writing with smaller font size

29. How can Lexile measures best help teachers and students choose texts to fit student abilities and interests?

a. By identifying the grade levels of many books and articles
b. By finding only texts exactly matching a student's number
c. By identifying text and student reading levels via numbers
d. By assigning a number to every book and article published

30. Which of the following choices is NOT an element of metacognition?

a. A reader's awareness of themselves as a learner
b. A reader's understanding of a variety of reading strategies
c. A reader who is conscious about remembering what has been read
d. A reader who can read with prosody

31. Which of the following best develops student oral vocabulary, spoken narrative skills, and connections between spoken and printed language?

a. Correctly spelling, pronouncing, and using new words in telling stories to the class
b. Learning new vocabulary words and spelling them correctly in written narratives
c. Learning new vocabulary words in listening, speaking, and storytelling activities
d. Correctly identifying new vocabulary words in listening and reading exercises

32. If a student has an assignment to speak before the whole class on a given topic and include a visual aid, which of the following technological tools would be most appropriate?

a. A slide show
b. A poster
c. A blog
d. A wiki

33. In the steps that a reader can follow to evaluate an informational text writer's arguments, which should come first?

a. Identifying the conclusion the argument makes
b. Judging the validity or supportiveness of premises
c. Clarifying premises or reasons with paraphrases
d. Identifying the supporting premises or reasons

34. How should a teacher initially plan instruction to meet the needs of a highly diverse classroom?

a. On the first day of class, the teacher should ask each student to complete a survey to determine the students' cultural, ethnic, and racial background.
b. A good teacher should be intimately familiar with the major cultures within the local school district.
c. A teacher should plan lessons so that new material is introduced using a variety of different approaches.
d. Guest teachers from different ethnic backgrounds should occasionally be invited to teach so that all students will feel more comfortable.

35. Which of the following choices will be most important when designing a reading activity or lesson for students?

a. Selecting a text
b. Determining the number of students participating
c. Analyzing the point in the school year at which the lesson is given
d. Determining a purpose for instruction

36. When students compare nonfiction literature to fictional literature, what differences will they generally find?

a. Nonfiction stories will be told in logical order and will relate only the facts, while fictional stories are never told in logical order.
b. Fictional stories include characters, settings, and themes, and nonfiction stories do not contain these elements.
c. Nonfiction stories tell about true events, characters, and settings from real life, whereas fictional stories are not based in reality.
d. Students will find few, if any, differences between these two types of literature because they are essentially the same.

37. A teacher plans to use a rubric to define learning objectives for a class instructional unit, guide students in completing their assignments, and serve as a unit assessment. Which statement is most applicable to incorporating student input into assessment design?

a. So many premade rubrics are available online, it is unnecessary to "reinvent the wheel."
b. Only the teacher, who knows learning objectives and how to do it, should create a rubric.
c. The teacher should collect student input on objectives and assignments to create a rubric.
d. The students and teacher should all work together in designing the rubric collaboratively.

38. The eighth-grade class will be holding class elections in the fall as part of an integrated Social Studies and English unit. The students will be studying government elections and modeling their process based on their studies. The candidates for Vice President and President will debate pre-determined issues in front of their class using modified rules found in formal debates (i.e. they are timed and will use a moderator). Which of the following exercises would be most beneficial to introduce in English class to help prepare each student for the debates?

a. Watch recordings of Presidential and Vice Presidential debates from years past and model their speech from what they have heard.
b. Create multiple opportunities for students to discuss the pre-determined issues in class, allowing for free-flowing dialogue and differing opinions.
c. Students write their thoughts in short-essay format so that each section can be read aloud during the appropriate part of the debate.
d. Students determine a position on each selected issue and assign it to a note card or small piece of paper. On each card, they record two to three reasons or supporting ideas for the opinion.

39. Which choice is the most correct statement about mood and tone in literature?

a. Mood and tone are synonyms referring to the emotional atmosphere of the work.
b. Mood is the emotion evoked in the reader by the work; tone is the author's emotion.
c. Mood is the emotion expressed by a work's author; tone is the emotion evoked in the reader by the work.
d. Mood is established by authors using different literary techniques than those used in creating tone.

40. Which of the following is true about children's writing skills?

a. Writing skills and reading skills reciprocally improve one another.
b. Writing skills are not apt to enhance learning as reading skills are.
c. Writing skills come naturally to children and need not be taught.
d. Writing skills meet any purpose or audience with the same style.

41. Which of the following statements is most accurate about writing the introduction of an essay?

a. The introduction should move from the broad and general to the focused and specific.
b. The introduction should save the most attention-getting material for later in the work.
c. The introduction should move from the focused and specific to the broad and general.
d. The introduction should use the technique of starting essays with dictionary definitions.

42. How are teachers required to ensure educational equity?

a. By delivering uniform instruction to all students
b. By offering different opportunities to students
c. By treating students less fairly if they deserve it
d. By using materials reflecting multicultural views

43. At one high school, a large proportion of ESL students are very recent immigrants to America. To help these students and their families understand the protocols and culture of the school better before the school year starts, the ESL teachers will host an orientation event. What should the teachers do first to enable understanding and present helpful information most effectively during this event?

a. They should provide families with a detailed analysis of the district ESL program.
b. They should ask the ESL students to function as interpreters with their families.
c. They should provide families with pertinent materials in their native languages.
d. They should arrange discussion groups for all families on their native languages.

44. Which statement is most accurate about social contexts of L1 and L2 acquisition?

a. L2 learning can occur equally in varied contexts, from natural to educational, but L1 learning cannot.
b. L1s are only learned in natural contexts, while L2s are learned in educational contexts.
c. Variations in L2 proficiency can result from the different contexts of the learning of L2s.
d. L2s are never learned in natural contexts, as they are not the learners' natural languages.

45. Mrs. Canas has had a parent offer to visit her fifth-grade class and provide a sign language seminar. The parent is fluent in American Sign Language and would like to offer her skills to benefit the students. Mrs. Canas thinks the seminar will be very interesting and provide a unique way to hone her students' listening and expressive skills. Which choice identifies another language skill set that would indirectly benefit from this seminar?

a. Students' understanding of how visual messages, including body language, facial expression, and signs inform verbal communication and ideas.
b. Students' fine motor skills and hand-eye coordination.
c. Students' respect for other cultures, specifically the non-hearing community.
d. Students' ability to communicate with other peers and adults in their community.

46. Which of these do experts advise teachers to do to be culturally responsive when interacting with linguistically diverse parents?

a. If the student is interpreting for his or her parents, the teacher should make eye contact with the student.
b. To show parents' educational importance to children, teachers must treat these parents as important.
c. When paperwork overwhelms parents, teachers should schedule meetings to aid them at later times.
d. Parents who speak conversational English fluently will not need help with filling out forms and paperwork.

47. Of the following, which is true about both *The Diary of a Young Girl* by Anne Frank (1947) and *Go Ask Alice* by Beatrice Sparks (1971), in addition to the fact that both are written in diary form?

a. They both are the diaries of 20th-century teenage girls.
b. They both are fictional novels created by the authors.
c. They both communicate negative perspectives on life.
d. They both end with the survival of the main character.

48. Which of the following instructional strategies would likely help students the most in understanding the difference between denotation and connotation and help them learn to identify the connotation of a word in context?

a. Providing example sentences in multiple choice questions asking for a word's connotation
b. Filling out a Venn diagram with sets of words that have connotations, denotations, or both
c. Assigning a reading where students identify and highlight words that have connotations
d. Giving word definitions and asking students to describe the feelings elicited by each definition

49. Which of the following is true regarding children's reading fluency?

a. The lack of reading fluency is always due to word-decoding deficits.
b. Children's motivation to read is unaffected by their reading fluency.
c. Some children need only more reading practice to develop fluency.
d. Fluency has equal impact on school performance at all grade levels.

50. Which of the following is the cognitive or learning objective of an assignment that asks students to "describe," "explain," "summarize," "restate," "classify," or "review" material they have read?

a. Knowledge recall
b. Application
c. Comprehension
d. Evaluation

51. Good books for a second-grader who is interested in reading fantasy fiction include:

a. *The BFG* and *Charlie and the Chocolate Factory*
b. *Harry Potter and the Sorcerer's Stone* and *The Golden Compass*
c. *Nate the Great* and *Amelia Bedelia*
d. *Commander Toad in Space* and *The Mouse and the Motorcycle*

52. Which of the following terms refers to description that activates the reader's senses?

a. Simile
b. Imagery
c. Metaphor
d. Hyperbole

53. A teacher has a child who does not volunteer in class. When the teacher asks the student a question the student can answer, she does so with as few words as possible. The teacher isn't sure how to best help the child. She should:

a. Leave the child alone. She is clearly very shy and will be embarrassed by having attention drawn to her. She is learning in her own way.
b. Ask two or three highly social children to include this girl in their activities. She is shy, and she probably won't approach them on her own.
c. Observe the child over the course of a week or two. Draw her into conversation and determine if her vocabulary is limited, if she displays emotional problems, or if her reticence could have another cause. Note how the child interacts with others in the class. Does she ever initiate conversation? If another child initiates, does she respond?
d. Refer her to the school counselor immediately. It is clear the child is suffering from either a low IQ or serious problems at home.

54. Which of the following aspects of poetic form is characteristic of haiku?

a. A 5-7-5 syllable pattern
b. An ABA rhyme scheme
c. Perfectly regular meter
d. Lengthy epic narratives

55. For a class with half native English-speaking students and half ELL students from various countries, what is the best way the teacher can promote intercultural understanding through reading?

a. Have the native English-speaking students read about other cultures, and have the ELLs read about mainstream culture.
b. Have all students read equal amounts of text that reflect both mainstream and other cultures.
c. Have the native English-speaking students read about mainstream culture, and have ELLs read about their own cultures.
d. Have all of these students choose the cultures they want to read about and the texts to read.

56. The school's English Department is looking to reform its curriculum to become more multicultural. Which would be the best step to take to accomplish this?

a. Including books that feature diverse characters from around the world
b. Participating in professional development to incorporate technology in the curriculum
c. Brainstorming guest speakers who can come to talk about culture
d. Focusing on validating students' cultural identities through redesigning units

57. Among the following, which form of assessment data can a teacher best use to review individual students' writing progress throughout an entire school year?

a. Reading assessments
b. Formative assessments
c. Summative assessments
d. Student writing portfolios

58. A teacher is working with a group of English language learners. She asks them to take two pieces of paper. At the top of the first paper, they are to write *SAME*, and at the top of the other, *DIFFERENT*. Each child will consider what his native country and the United States have in common, and what distinct features each country possesses. The children are using which method in organizing their ideas?

a. Hunt and peck
b. Consider and persuade
c. Evaluate and contrast
d. Compare and contrast

59. Which of the following is a good example of a learning goal that a teacher should set for a poetry unit in an English literature class?

a. Students will learn to identify the most common meters used in English literature, with a focus being placed upon iambic pentameter.
b. Students will learn to appreciate and enjoy poetry as an art form.
c. Students will learn how to identify the elements of good poetry.
d. Students will learn the cultural importance of poetry to English speakers around the world.

60. A teacher of a class with a wide range of backgrounds, reading levels, and reading skills wants to differentiate her lesson plans, instructional strategies, and assessment methods to meet every student's needs best. Which way of collecting information on their reading progress will best help her do this?

a. A whole-class test
b. Current Lexile levels
c. Small-group projects
d. Individual observations

61. A teacher gives students a story map to complete while reading a realistic fiction text. They are asked to record the characters, setting, problem, events, and solution. Which level of comprehension does this activity address?

a. Affective
b. Literal
c. Inferential
d. Evaluative

62. Principles of effective writing instruction include allotting enough time for systematic writing opportunities and teaching discourse knowledge (e.g., text structure, linguistic features). Among additional principles, which is most related to using writing to improve reading comprehension?

a. Differentiation among tiers
b. Explicit strategy instruction
c. Cross-curricular integration
d. Authentic writing activities

63. Which of the following approaches to writing instruction is characterized by setting clear writing goals, observing concrete data, and applying learning to written composition?

a. Prewriting strategies
b. Modeling strategies
c. Inquiry strategies
d. Process writing

64. A language arts teacher gives a five-question quiz over grammar using clickers once a week to her students. How could the teacher best utilize the data she can gather from these quizzes?

a. To determine which concepts to reteach by looking at the areas students most commonly missed
b. To replace the need for longer, more formal tests
c. To determine which students require special education services
d. To quantify the results of the teacher's instructional approach in a research study

65. The teacher provides students with a more advanced passage of reading, in which there are a variety of new words that many of the students do not know how to pronounce. How might the teacher go about helping the students in pronouncing the new words?

a. Hint at the correct pronunciation with a variety of different rhyming words
b. Assist the students in sounding out the words phonetically, by recognizing rules for vowels and consonants
c. Have the students look up the words in a dictionary to review the pronunciation information that is provided there
d. Ask students who are already familiar with the words to a help their classmates in pronouncing the new words

66. Studies evaluating instructional methods for language acquisition and vocabulary development have found which of the following?

a. Adding multimedia applications reduces learning gaps between ELL and other students.
b. Adding multimedia applications enhances learning equally for ELL and all other students.
c. Children have more difficulty recalling meanings of new words than their pronunciations.
d. Adding teacher questions and comments interferes with acquiring new word meanings.

67. Which of the following statements is correct regarding how teachers must respond to students' individual and group identities and needs in inclusive educational programs?

a. Teachers must meet student needs rather than student family needs.
b. Teachers must meet student needs but not express their own needs.
c. Teachers must meet their own needs through team problem-solving.
d. Teachers must meet their own needs through independent solutions.

68. What is the main role of literature, as described in the passage?

Throughout history, literature has served as a mirror to society, reflecting its joys, struggles, and complexities. Novels like *To Kill a Mockingbird* by Harper Lee shed light on issues of racial injustice, while George Orwell's *1984* explores the dangers of totalitarianism. These literary works continue to provide valuable insights into the human condition.

a. To entertain readers with fictional stories
b. To provide a glimpse into historical events
c. To reflect societal issues and human experiences
d. To promote the study of totalitarianism

69. The phrase "pretty as a picture" is best described as a:

a. Metaphor
b. Simile
c. Synecdoche
d. Paradox

70. Which of the following choices would be the least effective example of an integrated curriculum that includes language arts instruction?

a. Ms. Smith, a language teacher, confers with Mr. Langston, a history and social studies teacher. Ms. Smith shows Mr. Langston how to model previewing and predicting skills before he introduces a new unit or assignment so that the students build their comprehension skills while reading for information.
b. A science teacher recognizes that the students are having difficulty retaining information from their science textbooks when test time arrives. She creates a study guide with leading questions designed to help jog the students' memory about important concepts before the test.
c. Ms. Shannon, an art teacher, plans a field trip to see the latest exhibit featuring a symbolic artist. A language teacher at her school joins the students at the museum to lead a discussion about the function of symbols and their meanings, as well as different methods of interpreting shared symbols in a society.
d. A 1st-grade teacher uses children's books that introduce mathematical skills. For example, she reads a book weekly that tells a story about children preparing for a picnic, adding and subtracting items they need for the trip along the way. She encourages the children to solve the math questions along with her during the story.

71. The teacher and her students brainstorm a list of talents, skills, and specialized knowledge belonging to members of the class. Some of the items on the list include how to make a soufflé, how to juggle, and how to teach a dog to do tricks. One student knows a great deal about spiders, and another knows about motorcycles. The teacher asks the students to each write an essay about something they are good at or know a great deal about. What kind of essay is she asking the students to produce?

a. Cause and effect
b. Compare/contrast
c. Expository
d. Argumentative

72. To provide accommodations for ELL students, which of these should teachers do in vocabulary and reading instruction?

a. Teach ELL students vocabulary in isolation.
b. Teach ELL students vocabulary in context.
c. Teach ELL students vocabulary in volume.
d. Teach ELL students reading by their speech levels.

73. Which of the following is NOT a goal of children's literature?

a. Focus on choices, morals, and values.
b. Instruct students through entertaining stories.
c. Promote an interest in reading itself.
d. Instruct students in the sciences, such as mathematics and biology.

74. "Language load" refers to:

a. The basic vocabulary words a first grader has committed to memory.
b. The number of unrecognizable words an English language learner encounters when reading a passage or listening to a teacher.
c. The damage that carrying a pile of heavy books could cause to a child's physique.
d. The number of different languages a person has mastered

75. What have studies found about how teachers interpret and apply research to reading instruction challenges?

a. Teachers make data-based instructional decisions better individually than in small groups.
b. Teachers are generally better at data comprehension than data location in graphs or tables.
c. Teachers do far better at interpreting relationships among variables than question-posing.
d. Teachers plan differentiated instruction better with real (not hypothetical) student scores.

76. William Shakespeare wrote during which historical and literary period?

a. Medieval
b. Renaissance
c. Restoration
d. Enlightenment

77. In research fields, what does *literature* mean?

a. All the written works in a language
b. The profession of a writer or author
c. All existing research on a subject
d. Any kind of printed materials

78. In Kate Chopin's short story "The Story of an Hour" (1894), Chopin's description of Louise Mallard as "young, with a fair, calm face, whose lines bespoke repression and even a certain strength" contributes to her character development to help explain which plot event most?

a. Her reaction to seeing her husband alive.
b. The controlling behavior of her husband.
c. Why her immediate grief ended so soon.
d. Her joy when her husband was not dead.

Refer to the following for question 79:

Valeria is a bright sixth-grader who struggles with reading fluency. She comes from a predominantly Spanish-speaking home and has only lived in the United States for two years. Her teacher plans to use the guided oral reading strategy to help increase Valeria's reading skills. She also plans to use Valeria's scheduled media time to help work on her fluency.

79. Which of the following computer activities/games would be most beneficial to use during Valeria's media time?

a. Valeria can select from a variety of high-interest texts and read aloud what she sees on the screen.
b. Valeria can hear high-frequency sight and vocabulary words in her headphones and get points for "zapping" (clicking) the correct matching word on her screen.
c. Valeria can practice typing in a keyboarding program to build her speed and accuracy in writing reports and papers.
d. Valeria can surf a limited and pre-approved number of internet sites to read on subjects of her choosing.

80. A history teacher discusses the structure of nonfiction texts by explaining the text structures of comparison and contrast, cause and effect, problem and solution, and chronological order. Which text structure do the following chapter titles from *A Textbook of the History of Architecture* represent?

CHAPTER I: PRIMITIVE AND PREHISTORIC ARCHITECTURE
CHAPTER X: .EARLY CHRISTIAN ARCHITECTURE
CHAPTER XIII: EARLY MEDIAEVAL ARCHITECTURE IN ITALY AND FRANCE
CHAPTER XX: EARLY RENAISSANCE ARCHITECTURE IN ITALY
CHAPTER XXVII: ARCHITECTURE IN THE UNITED STATES

a. comparison and contrast
b. cause and effect
c. chronological order
d. problem and solution

81. The English teacher read a passage from contemporary YA novel that shows a student's conflict with her mother. The main character, Beth, takes a stand against her mother's demand that she participate in art rather than in science, her main interest. The teacher asked the students to remember a similar conflict they had with a parent or a sibling and write a brief paragraph about how they felt.

This exercise would address which of the following instructional goals?

a. Encourage students to use writing as a means for personal exploration and self-expression.
b. Encourage students to disagree with their parents or siblings on issues that might be important to them.
c. Encourage students to understand the structure of a contemporary novel.
d. Encourage students to understand how a plot is developed through conflict.

82. A teacher assigns a project in which students must compare excerpts from the Charles Dickens novel they are reading in class and an article from the week's newspaper. The teacher has chosen a specific passage from the novel. The students can choose the newspaper excerpts, as long as they are of similar lengths. The students must then write a short essay comparing the two. What is this teacher hoping to show her students?

a. That Dickens' writing style is journalistic and that he informed much of what is considered to be current journalistic philosophy.
b. That there are links between the students' lives and what they read in class; the relationships are there if they make an effort to see them.
c. That you can compare even two unlike things.
d. That there are distinct differences between the way meaning is constructed in daily life and in literature; different processes must be applied.

83. Which choice is the best method of structuring language arts curriculum and instruction?

a. Examine all state-level or national standardized tests that students will be required to take. Structure the curriculum and lessons to address all concepts included in the tests, with an attempt to proportion the time spent in a way that mirrors the breakdown of the tests.
b. Research the instructional methods used in supplemental education fields. Use those newer methods of introducing and reinforcing concepts in class to ensure that students are receiving consistent and standard instruction.
c. Use the written curriculum provided by the school district or specific campus as a foundation for instruction. Schedule regular planning sessions to incorporate a variety of texts and instruction methods, as well as to coordinate instruction with teachers of other subjects.
d. Plan sequential units of study that focus on isolated skills such as word and vocabulary study, comprehension strategies, listening, viewing, and speaking. Design lessons to focus on the mastery of one skill at a time with the goal of studying the relationship between skills toward the end of the school year.

84. In writing instruction, what does the process writing approach entail?

a. Hypothetical audiences for written work
b. Students work on their own throughout.
c. Personal responsibility for written work
d. Writing is evaluated only by the teacher.

85. Which of the following is NOT an English Language Arts expectation for middle school students in the English Language Arts subject area?

a. To interpret and understand visual imagery, meanings, and messages
b. To conduct analyses and critiques of how visual media are important
c. To produce visual media representations communicating with others
d. To get ideas from the environment, and develop and organize them

86. Which of these accurately reflects influences on media choices for giving presentations?

a. Combining more than one type of media is advisable.
b. Experts find it more effective to limit presentations to one medium.
c. Presenters should not let their budgets influence their choice.
d. The length of communication will not affect the media.

87. When writing an essay, which is the best way to address multiple main points?

a. Write a separate paragraph for each point, including the point's supporting evidence and its relation to the thesis.
b. Introduce each point in one paragraph, support it in another, and relate it to the thesis in another.
c. Cover all main points, supporting evidence, and their connections with thesis in one long paragraph.
d. Address each main point in a logical order using any number of paragraphs necessary for readability.

88. Based on research evidence, what do experts recommend to effectively instruct students in writing strategies?

a. Teachers should demonstrate strategies and then assign independent student practice.
b. Teachers should explain strategies and let students practice them without any models.
c. Teachers should model strategies, then guide practice, then give independent practice.
d. Teachers should first give students guided practice in strategies and then model them.

89. If a teacher assigns students to pairs for cooperative writing partnerships, which of the following should their activities include?

a. One student should write, and the other should review the work.
b. Each partner in a pair takes turns being the writer and the reviewer.
c. Each student should provide only positive feedback to the other.
d. Each student should give only constructive feedback to the other.

90. Cognates and realia are most useful for teaching which component of reading instruction to ELLs?

a. Vocabulary
b. Prosody
c. Phonological awareness
d. Phonemic awareness

Answer Key and Explanations for Test #1

1. C: The fact that digital networking enables educators and learners to communicate nearly instantly with a variety of experts, mentors, and peers all over the world has transformed the social interactions available in the educational community. Additional advantages of digital networking include that digital educational resources can be linked to one another; that embedded hyperlinks afford students easy access to learning supports like electronic notepads, graphic organizers, supplementary information, reading comprehension prompts, encyclopedias, dictionaries and thesauruses, and more; and that the diversity of digital formats available provide experiences more similar in their diversity to that of individual students. These advantages are all transformative of learning itself. Access to global communications is an advantage transformative specifically of social interactions (including remote and long-distance) within the learning process, as well as of learning.

2. B: How appropriate the content of a student's composition is reflects function rather than form. Composition length (A), word usage (C), and spelling (D) in a student's composition are all reflections of the composition's form rather than its function.

3. B: Assessment is an ongoing process that involves formal testing and a host of other methods. Students are working at any given time in the school year on a multitude of skill sets, and all of these skills are interrelated and developing simultaneously at different rates. It is difficult to provide a complete "snapshot" of a student's abilities, because each student develops in a unique and complex manner. Choice A would only offer insight into a student's reading fluency. Choice C would show how a student could perform on standardized tests; however, many factors such as anxiety and test-taking speed affect those scores. Choice D relies on the teacher to interpret the student's strengths and weaknesses and would require an almost impossible attention to detail. Choice B includes both formal and informal assessments as well as giving insight into writing, vocabulary and other skill sets in a comprehensive portfolio.

4. D: This description matches that of a typical peer review, so (D) is correct. In a peer review, writers read a peer's paper and then identify values in it, describe it, ask questions about it, and suggest points for revision. These types of feedback have been identified by experts as helpful for writing. (A) and (C) are incorrect because these types of reviews are not typically collaborative. For a portfolio assessment (A), the teacher collects finished work products from a student over time, eventually assembling a portfolio of work. Holistic scoring (C) is a method of scoring a piece of writing for overall quality (evaluating general elements such as focus, organization, support, and conventions) rather than being overly concerned with any individual aspect of writing. While a writing workshop (B) may be collaborative, it may or may not include a peer review session, and the main motivation for attending a writing workshop is generally not for the peer feedback but for professional guidance, as from a coach or editor, and to build a professional network.

5. B: For a variety of reasons, students' families may be reluctant to actively participate in their children's education program. This could be due to previous negative experiences with the school, lack of confidence in their ability to meaningfully contribute, or uncertainty regarding ways to participate. By providing multiple opportunities for family involvement, teachers can encourage families to participate in the education program in a way that best suits their needs, abilities, and lifestyle demands. Doing so helps to ensure that all families feel welcomed and included as valued participants in their children's learning.

6. B: Explicit and systematic phonics instruction involves planning the teaching of specific phonics skills in a logical order, from simplest to most complex, using a part-to-whole approach. It requires understanding students' existing phonics knowledge and planning instruction to address specific skills that they still need to develop. Choice A and choice D demonstrate implicit phonics instruction, where students read whole texts, and phonics instruction occurs based on students' struggles and/or observations as they read. It uses a whole-to-part approach. Choice C involves preplanned phonics instruction, but the teacher is selecting phonics skills to address based on the content of the books rather than a research-based sequencing of skills from simplest to most complex.

7. B: The first thing a researcher should look for in a review of the existing literature related to a specific research question is whether that question has already been definitively answered. If so, the researcher should ask a different research question. If the question has not already been answered conclusively, then the researcher can look for gaps in knowledge about the topic that searching the literature reveals; review the literature to find what needs and opportunities for further research other researchers have identified; examine the literature to discern whether there is consensus, controversy, or both; and if so, what those opinions are about the topic. These considerations help inform the direction for research.

8. D: Teachers are expected to give students plenty of opportunities not only to read different literary genres independently (A), but also to listen to literature read aloud (B), to attend or view productions of dramatic literature, to express their responses to literature in writing and speech (C), and to interact with others (D) in class and group discussions, pairs, cooperative learning projects, conversations, etc.

9. D: The purpose of narrative writing (A) is to entertain readers with a story. Even when authors want to offer insights or teach lessons while entertaining readers, they accomplish this through storytelling. The purpose of expository writing (B) is to inform or direct readers. The purpose of persuasive writing (C) is to convince readers to agree with the author's position or argument. The purpose of speculative writing (D) is to encourage readers to explore ideas and potential responses rather than entertain, tell stories, inform, explain, direct, or convince.

10. C: Good essay organization has many benefits. First, good organization makes the reader more likely to accept the validity of the writer's thesis, making choice A incorrect. Good organization also helps to keep the reader's attention, so choice B is incorrect. Since well-organized essays typically follow a standard format, identifying main ideas is usually easier for readers, which makes choice D incorrect. Choice C is correct because good organization requires more effort from the writer, but it results in easier understanding for the reader.

11. D: Predicting what (like a quest or a war) or whom (such as a prince or three animals) a book is about is a common practice of students who fall back on the easiest answer to a teacher's request to make predictions. It is more useful for teachers to challenge students to try to predict what a character in a novel will do or a significant event that may occur in a story. Teachers can explain to students that they can make predictions by looking for clues in book titles, front-cover illustrations, and illustrations inside a book before even reading it. They can also have students read just one passage from a book, and then have them predict what will occur next.

12. C: When reading independently, students are at the correct level if they read with at least 97% accuracy.

13. C: Authors who normally write informational text will often need to develop proposals that communicate the value of projects to those unfamiliar with the technicalities, so choice C is the correct answer. Moreover, they may need to communicate simpler, clearer messages rather than dense content, meaning choice A is incorrect. Professionals in relevant fields would likely be familiar enough with the subject matter to understand technical language, while experts in the subject are unlikely to need nontechnical explanations at all, making choices B and D incorrect.

14. A: Critiques of final projects (e.g., art projects, research projects, music recitals) are examples of summative assessments because they measure student achievement following instruction. Oral question-and-answer sessions (b) are examples of formative assessments because they can be brief, can be administered often, and can be used to monitor ongoing student progress. Running records (c) keep track of student performance in real time (e.g., oral reading fluency) and are also formative assessments. Pop quizzes (d) are typically short, may be given at any time, and cover the most recent information during instruction; thus, they are also examples of formative assessments.

15. B: The evidence in this selection indicates that marrying a man with money was a primary goal for young women. Mrs. Bennet tells Mr. Bennet that Mr. Bingley is "A single man of large fortune; four or five thousand a year." Mrs. Bennet further indicates that she is thrilled with the news because of Mr. Bingley's potential as a husband for one of her daughters: "What a fine thing for our girls... You must know that I am thinking of his marrying one of them."

16. A: The process of actively constructing meaning from reading is interactive, in that it involves the text itself, the person reading it, and the setting in which the reading is done. These three elements influence each other, and this is the concept indicated by the term *interactive* in the question, so choice A is correct. Choice B is a better definition of the *strategic* aspect of the process. Choice C and Choice D are better definitions of the *adaptable* aspect of the process.

17. D: A speech differs from an essay in that it is spoken or read aloud to a live audience, where as an essay is published. Because speeches are given at live events, certain components may need to be included that would not be necessary or appropriate in an essay. These components include greetings (to the audience and possibly to honored guests) and thanks (perhaps to the audience for listening or perhaps to those who have helped or influenced the speaker). Therefore, choice D is correct. Choice A is incorrect because speech introductions differ from essay introductions in that they may include some of the elements above. Choice B is incorrect because the body of a speech and the body of an essay should elaborate and provide supporting evidence in a similar fashion. Choice C is incorrect because speech conclusions, while they sometimes need to include information that essay conclusions do not, must be appropriately forceful and engaging, just as essay conclusions should be.

18. D: When readers visualize, they use the clues and details in the stories to form mental pictures in their minds. When students draw a setting based on how they imagined it from the description in the story, they are visualizing. Predicting refers to making guesses about the text before reading. Inferring refers to using clues in the story to determine the meaning when it is not explicitly stated. Summarizing refers to retelling the main events of the story.

19. A: Research finds one helpful instructional strategy for ELL student language acquisition is to have them explain and/or retell what the teacher just said to their classmates. This not only ensures their comprehension, but it also gives them practice analyzing the English they hear, restating/paraphrasing English, and communicating to others in spoken English. Teachers should incorporate visual aids: studies show supplementing verbal input visually helps ELLs understand concepts in subject content areas as they are learning a foreign language. Research finds that students cannot grasp abstract concepts as readily in a foreign language, so teachers should give them concrete objects, pictures, and the like to illustrate and demonstrate ideas as students gradually transition from concrete to abstract in a new language. Teachers can arrange for ELLs to signal when they don't understand; they also closely observe ELLs, and if they do not indicate or demonstrate understanding, they should elaborate by summarizing, paraphrasing, and giving synonyms.

20. C: One-half of the class receives signs showing vocabulary words, which are probably used as root words. The remaining students are split into two general groups: those with prefixes on their signs and those with suffixes. The best approach is to get the students moving, listening, and talking in order to solidify their understanding of how roots, suffixes, and prefixes work together to make new meanings out of various root words. This approach also allows the students to participate in a game in a group context, making the activity more fun and engaging.

21. C: Oral language skills can be distinguished from specific speech characteristics exhibited by some children. Many students like Rosa, whose first language is not English, will speak with an accent and may be less clear when speaking about a topic that is unfamiliar. In fact, even those who are not English Language Learners may exhibit difficulty speaking on new topics. Greer may avoid oral assignments or speaking in class for a number of reasons, such as self-consciousness. This student could be helped by evaluating oral language skills in a one-on-one environment or by introducing peer scaffolding to help reduce anxiety. Brett's demeanor in group assignments may also be due to social characteristics rather than oral skills; it would be important to evaluate his skills in various contexts. Ashley, however, shows marked problems communicating orally both in class discussion and in prepared assignments. She would benefit from specific instruction related to presenting ideas orally.

22. A: Anticipating objections (A) involves addressing, dismissing, or attempting to refute opposing arguments against the author's views that the reader might think of or hear. Testimonials (D), such as anecdotes or quotations, support an author's views by showing readers that other people agree. Citing expert opinions (B) supports an author's views by showing readers that a knowledgeable authority on the subject agrees. Bandwagon appeals (C) support an author's views by showing readers that the mainstream agrees.

23. C: Citing evidence of only one budget cut (A), even though it is the largest, is not sufficient evidence because it does not represent a significant proportion of all community colleges in the state. Similarly, citing only two examples (B), regardless of their prominence, does not represent a significant proportion of the total. Citing examples from 15 of 34 colleges (C) in the state shows that the general claim is true for a significant proportion of community colleges in the state. Citing specific cut amounts at all 34 colleges (D) is beyond sufficient, to the point of excess: reading/listening audiences would likely be so bored by this amount of evidence, it would distract them from accepting the claim.

24. D: Word roots, prefixes, and suffixes are all morphological units, i.e., the smallest structural or grammatical units of words that carry meaning (e.g., the *–s* ending added to regular nouns changes them from singular to plural in number, and the *–ed* ending added to regular verbs changes them from present to past tense). Identifying morphological word parts gives students structural cues to determine word meaning. Alphabetic principle knowledge (A) is the knowledge that letters correspond to speech sounds. Combining vowel sounds (B) enables word decoding by using alphabetic principle knowledge and phonics to connect combinations of vowel letters with their combined sounds. Semantic and syntactic context (C) enables decoding unknown words by considering the meaning of the semantic context (surrounding phrase, sentence, paragraph, etc.) and the surrounding syntactic context (sentence structure and word order).

25. A: The article provides information about a scheme to defraud internet users of money. It describes the mechanics of the fraud scheme and explains how the perpetrators intend to make money.

26. B: Teachers should base rubrics on their identified lesson objectives. They should explain a rubric to students in advance, and have students refer to the rubric as a guide while they work. Teachers should then use the rubric to assess whether students have met all included learning objectives. Rubrics can be used as both formative and summative assessment tools, meaning they were assessed either during or after the work, respectively. Rubrics are not replacements for clearly stating learning goals, objectives, expectations, and teacher modeling of expected performance: teachers should do all of these to enable optimal student performance, as well as supply a rubric to guide and assess student work. Teachers should also make very clear to students the relationship between learning goals and their performance.

27. C: A good summary of text captures the main ideas, omitting the details and other less important information. A summary does not literally retell the text or repeat it word for word. It shows reader comprehension by paraphrasing the major meaning of the text in the reader's own words.

28. A: Bloggers need to use correct punctuation to encourage continued reading of their posts. If they are not already confident in their grasp of punctuation, they should write in shorter sentences until they are. Because reading on computer screens is harder than on paper, paragraphs in blogs must be significantly shorter than in print, not longer. Shorter paragraphs enable readers to "chunk" the information. Font sizes should be larger rather than smaller to be easier on readers' eyes and more legible onscreen.

29. C: Lexile measures assign numbers to many books and articles that identify their reading levels, from below 200L to above 1700L. These are reading levels not to be confused with grade levels. Students can also be assigned Lexile measure numbers through their scores on standardized reading tests they may be given in school. Teachers and students can select texts that correspond to a range around a student's Lexile measure; 50L above and 100L below the student's number is a recommended range. Lexile measures do not find these texts; teachers and/or students do. They are not advised to find only texts exactly matching a student's number, as this would overly restrict available reading material and is unnecessary. Students can generally read and enjoy texts in a range around their level. Lexile measures are not assigned to every book and article published; over 80 million articles and over 100,000 books have Lexile measure numbers, providing identification of ample reading matter for those wishing to use this system.

30. D: Prosody is not an element of metacognition. Metacognition means a reader's awareness of their own reading processes as they improve reading comprehension. Other elements of metacognition include awareness of areas in the text that the reader does not comprehend and an understanding of how the text is structured.

31. A: Learning correct spelling and pronunciation of new vocabulary words develops student connections between spoken and printed language; using the new words in telling stories to the class develops student spoken narrative skills. Option B develops vocabulary and written language skills but not necessarily oral vocabulary. It also does not address spoken narrative skills or spoken-printed language connections. Option C develops oral language and narrative skills but does not address spoken-printed language connections. Option D addresses receptive vocabulary recognition and receptive connections between spoken and printed language but not expressive oral vocabulary, expressive spoken-printed language production, or spoken narrative skills.

32. A: A slide show presentation is designed as a visual aid to summarize and highlight the main points in a speaker's talk. Slide show presentation slides commonly feature brief verbal phrases and sentences; are often numbered or bulleted; and also may include pictures, diagrams, graphs, and more. The slides not only visualize the speaker's main points for audiences, guide listeners through the presentation, and facilitate note-taking and outlining by listeners, they also help keep the speaker organized and on the subject. The slides provide an outline of the presentation; the speaker supplies the additional details. A poster is a visual aid, but not a technological tool. It would also not add as much to the presentation as a slide show. A blog and a wiki are both designed for audiences to read online, not to read while someone is speaking or to listen to someone reading them aloud.

33. A: The first step a reader should take in evaluating the arguments in an informational text is to identify the conclusion the author draws with the argument. The second step is to identify what premises or reasons support this conclusion. The third step is to clarify these premises or reasons by paraphrasing them in the reader's own words, which can also show whether the premises fit with the conclusion they should support. The reader can then list all premises in order, followed by the conclusion, and note any assumptions or premises necessary to support the conclusion that the author may have omitted. The next step is judging whether a deductive reasoning argument is valid, or whether an inductive reasoning argument uses true premises that support the conclusion.

34. C: Introducing new material using several different strategies will help make it more accessible to a larger group of students, regardless of their specific backgrounds. While surveys and general knowledge about cultures may be useful, relying too much on generalized beliefs about cultures and what they value and find useful in instruction can be problematic.

35. D: It is impossible to include every text desired into the language curriculum—there are simply too many good books, stories, poems, speeches, and media available. Teachers must first think about what skills their students need to acquire, as well as what skills they have already mastered. In designing activities for class, a good teacher will start first with the purpose for instruction. For example, purposes of reading can include: reading for information, reading for enjoyment, understanding a message, identifying main or supporting ideas, or developing an appreciation for artistic expression/perception. Once the purpose or intended learning outcome has been identified, the teacher will have a much better idea of which texts, strategies, and activities will support that purpose.

36. C: Nonfiction works are distinguished by the intention to be factual works, even when biases or interpretation of events are included. Nonfiction works do not only tell stories, but many do. In addition to plot, character, setting, and theme, a nonfiction story may also include interpretations, theories, and research. For example, a biography is a type of nonfiction work that has many elements of a story. In addition, it may introduce interpretations and theories related to the subject's life and actions and show the author's research. The main identifier of nonfiction is that it intends to only tell stories about real life. While fictional stories do not always describe real events, they can be realistic, based on real events, and clearly based in reality. Fiction does not have to be grounded in reality or tell true stories. Fiction exists on a greater spectrum and can use real characters, events, or settings and simply change elements to something factually incorrect to become fiction. This can be something realistic or unrealistic. For example, a story about Martin Luther set in 16th-century Germany would be nonfiction if based on factual events. However, if the author included Abraham Lincoln as a character, having the two historical figures from different times interacting, it would become fiction because it introduces an element that is historically impossible.

37. D: Although there are many ready-made rubrics available online free of charge, and a teacher's selecting one this way eliminates added work (A), it does nothing to incorporate student input. Although the teacher knows the learning objectives and how to create a rubric, the teacher is not the only one who should do it (B): collaborating with students will not only ensure that they know and understand the learning objectives as well as teach them how to design rubrics, but it will also incorporate their input and feedback about curriculum and assessment into the design. Rather than collecting student input and then creating the rubric alone (C), the teacher should work together with all students to incorporate their input (D).

38. D: In the debate process, it is important for students to take a position and support it with evidence or arguments in order to make their claims effective. Choice "d" requires students to formulate their opinions and supporting arguments, and helps them reduce extraneous information and create "reminders" for their talking points on notecards. Choice "c" requires students to prepare their arguments but encourages reading aloud during the debate rather than actually speaking directly to their opponent or to the crowd. Choice "c" fails to help students distinguish between written language and oral language and their occasionally separate purposes. Choice "b" creates opportunities for informal debate, but does not teach students the parameters for formal debating. Choice "a" is similarly informal and does not familiarize students with the preparation process with respect to formulating arguments, opinions, or preparing to speak in front of a large audience.

39. B: Mood refers to the emotions evoked in the reader by the literary work, whereas tone refers to the emotions or attitude of the author toward the subject matter or audience, making choice B correct. Choice C is the reverse of this, so it is not correct. Choice A is incorrect because mood and tone do not mean the same thing. Though mood and tone have different meanings, neither one is associated with particular techniques; the same literary techniques could be used for either purpose, so choice D is incorrect.

40. A: Literacy research shows that reading and writing development have mutual benefits: improving one improves the other, and vice versa. Researchers find that children's capacity to learn is increased by increases in *both* reading and writing skills (B). Educational researchers have also found that to write well, children must have instruction; it is not a skill set that comes naturally to them (C). It is not true that having good writing skills enables the writer to meet any purpose or audience using the same single writing style (D): a part of learning writing skills is learning the ability to vary one's style and write in different genres to suit different purposes (e.g., to persuade, to inform, to amuse, or to express ideas and feelings) and different intended audiences (e.g., using different language, tone, and references that are relevant to and appeal to different readers).

41. A: An introduction should move from broad, general statements about a topic to a focused and specific point regarding the topic. This point is the thesis statement. While the strongest points should come later in the body of an essay, the most attention-grabbing statements should be those in the introduction, as these will serve to engage the reader's interest in the topic and in reading the rest of the essay. Therefore, choice B is incorrect. Starting with focused and specific statements followed by broad and general statements is the opposite of how an introduction should be structured, so choice C is incorrect. Writing experts advise that the technique of beginning an essay with a dictionary definition has become overused and should therefore be avoided, so choice D is incorrect.

42. D: Answer D is correct because the use of multicultural materials supports equity by reflecting diverse perspectives to which multicultural students can relate. Answer A is incorrect because uniform instruction ignores diverse needs and varying student abilities. Answer B is incorrect because offering different opportunities alone does not guarantee equity unless those opportunities are intentionally aligned to students' needs and goals. Answer C is incorrect because treating students less fairly is never appropriate.

43. C: By providing recent immigrant families with materials pertinent to the orientation in their native languages, the teachers will ensure that the families understand the content of the materials. Providing the families with a detailed analysis of the district ESL program (A) will not give them an understanding of all of the school's protocols and culture, but of only one component. Asking the ESL students to interpret for their families (B) does not acknowledge that many of these recent immigrant students may not have the English-language proficiency to interpret, and doing so could activate the students' affective filters. Arranging discussion groups about the families' native languages (D) can promote communication among these families, but it will not help students' parents understand the information the teachers are presenting to them during the orientation event.

44. C: Second languages can be learned in a number of educational contexts. For example, they can be segregated from the L1, formally taught via the medium of the L1, taught through submersion, or taught within the language classroom but not used to communicate outside of it. The L2 can also be learned in several natural contexts. Because of these variations, L2 learners may acquire different elements of the language or may vary in how much of the language they acquire, so choice C is correct. Just like an L2, an L1 can also be learned in an education or natural context, so choice A is incorrect. While many L1s are learned naturally at first, they are learned in educational contexts as well, so choice B is incorrect. Just like L1s, L2s can be learned and used naturally, so choice D is incorrect.

45. A: If you read the question prompt carefully, you will notice that the question refers specifically to language skills. While Choice "c" is important and would likely result from the exercise, it does not signify a specific language skill. Students' motor skills are not likely to significantly improve over the course of one day, eliminating Choice "b". In Choice "d", the assumption that other individuals in the community would be able to interpret sign language is incorrect. But the seminar would indeed provide an opportunity for students to learn about how visual representations affect meaning. Using sign language allows them to hone listening and expression skills simultaneously, as well as to learn how to decode nonverbal expressions.

46. B: In some situations, it is acceptable for students to interpret for their parents. In these cases, experts advise teachers to make eye contact with the parent(s), not the interpreting child (A). To show immigrant parents the importance of their role in their children's education, teachers themselves must treat the parents as important (B) by honoring and respecting them. Experts advise teachers to help parents overwhelmed by paperwork immediately, not later (C). This includes parents who converse fluently in English (D), who often are not equally adept with formal printed English.

47. A: Both books are diaries of 20th-century teenage girls. However, while Beatrice Sparks created a fictional plot and characters in her novel using diary format, Anne Frank's diary is nonfiction, written by a real person (B). The fictional Alice develops a somewhat negative perspective on life through her experiences (e.g., she is left with permanent neurological damage), she returns home and hopes for a better life. Anne Frank's entries, on the other hand, convey a markedly positive attitude despite horrific realities (C). The fictional Alice survives; following Frank's last, optimistic entry, an epilogue reports her death soon after (D).

48. A: An effective way to teach students the difference between denotation and connotation is to provide example sentences and have students choose a given word that best expresses the connotation of a highlighted word in each sentence. For example, to show the connotation of the word *challenge*, an example sentence "This is one of the many challenges that must be faced in order to solve the problem" could be given, and students could choose whether the connotation suggested by "challenges" in this case was "threats," "obstacles," "criticisms," or "setbacks." This instructional strategy is summarized in choice A, which is the correct answer. Since words generally have denotations and may or may not have connotations depending on their use, a Venn diagram would be misleading, and choice B is incorrect. Choice C is also incorrect, as highlighting words in a passage would not require students to distinguish between denotations and connotations, nor even to identify the exact connotations of words in context. Choice D would not be logical, since not all words have an emotional connotation, and the definition alone will be of little use for determining the connotations of a specific use of a word.

49. C: While *some* children's reading lacks fluency due to deficits in their word-decoding abilities, this is not *always* (A) the case: some children simply need more reading practice to develop fluency. Children's motivation to read (B) *is* affected by their reading fluency: when reading is laborious, children do not enjoy it and avoid reading; when reading is easy, children enjoy it and want to read. Fluency has much *greater* impact (D) on the performance of students in higher grades, when the volume of reading required of them in school is exponentially greater.

50. C: Choice C is correct, since the verbs mentioned in the question all refer to interpreting information in one's own words—which involves the cognitive objective of comprehension. Tasks targeting knowledge recall (A) would ask students to name, label, list, define, repeat, memorize, order, or arrange material. Tasks targeting application (B) would ask students to calculate, solve, practice, operate, sketch, use, prepare, illustrate, or apply material. Tasks targeting evaluation (D) would ask students to judge, appraise, evaluate, conclude, predict, score, or compare material.

51. D: These books by Jane Yolen and Beverly Cleary are fantasies that are written for children who read at a typical second-grade level. The books included in choices A and B are too difficult for second-grade students. The titles in choice C are good examples of realistic fiction.

52. B: Imagery is description that activates readers' senses so they can more clearly imagine what is described. For example, in the poem *The Waste Land,* T. S. Eliot conveys a civilization's decay through images of dried-up wells, crumbling towers, and toppled tombstones. A simile is an explicit comparison using *like* or *as*, such as William Wordsworth's famous line "I wandered lonely as a cloud." A metaphor is an implicit comparison. In a metaphor, the writer equates one thing to another. The reader is expected to understand that it is a comparison and not to be taken literally. Hyperbole deliberately exaggerates for effect, as in Mark Twain's line "I ... could have hung my hat on my eyes, they stuck out so far." Although simile, metaphors, and hyperbole can be used in imagery, they do not always use description to activate the reader's senses, such as in the metaphor "time is money."

53. C: Until the teacher monitors the child's verbal abilities and habits, she cannot determine if the lack of interaction suggests a learning disability, an emotional problem, or simply a shy personality. The teacher should informally observe the child over a period of time, noting if and when she initiates or responds to oral language, if she is reading with apparent comprehension, if her vocabulary is limited, and the degree to which the child is interested in understanding.

54. A: The haiku, originating in Japanese poetry and since adopted in English-language poetry, is a short poem of only three lines, often with 17 syllables, with the first and third lines having five syllables and the second line having seven syllables. (In Japanese there are many other rules, which become complicated in comparison to the English version.) Because this syllable pattern is a defining characteristic of English-language haiku, choice A is correct. Haiku are typically unrhymed, so they do not have a rhyme scheme (B). Similarly, they do not employ any regular meter (C). Because haiku are typically 17 syllables or fewer, they do not involve long narratives (D).

55. B: The best way to promote intercultural understanding among students through reading is to have all students read equal amounts of text reflecting the mainstream culture and the other cultures from which the ELL students come. Option (A) would certainly expose all students to cultures other than their own, but it would not enable all students to read about both mainstream and other cultures. Option (C) would not expose either student group to cultures other than their own. Though it is important to give students some choice in reading materials, leaving text selection entirely up to students (D) cannot ensure variety or balance, let alone equity, and also deprives students of teacher guidance in selecting reading matter.

56. D: Validating cultural identities of the students is a great step toward creating a multicultural curriculum. Although Answer A is an excellent strategy for schools to undertake, it would not be as effective as reworking the curriculum at a more fundamental level. Professional development is also another key aspect of changing a curriculum; however, Answer B focuses on technology rather than on teacher cultural self-reflection or understanding the various cultures in the United States. Guest speakers are also a great asset to building a multicultural curriculum, but these are often one-off events, which can be more surface level.

57. D: Reading assessments (A) are necessary components of a comprehensive writing assessment system because writing depends on reading, but they will not show yearlong individual student writing progress. Formative assessments (B) will each show student progress at a given time during the year, not throughout it. Summative assessments (C) will show what the student can achieve by the end of the year. Teachers can best review yearlong individual writing progress through student writing goals and samples collected in student writing portfolios (D), aligned with instruction.

58. D: Asking children to write a list provides them with a visual model that is a side-by-side comparison of the two countries. In creating that visual model, each student first has to organize his or her thoughts mentally, deciding whether each particular item under consideration is shared between both countries or is a difference between them.

59. A: This is a specific, practical goal that can be taught, tested, and evaluated. Answer B is ambiguous, and it cannot be effectively evaluated. Answer C sounds specific but in fact deals in opinion. What makes a poem good is a subjective matter about which people disagree. Answer D is also ambiguous. The learning goals for each unit should be specific and measurable.

60. D: Of the choices given, the best way to get information for differentiating instruction for individual students is through observations of individual students (D) with detailed observational notes of their specific reading needs and strengths. A whole-class test (A) will yield different individual student scores and even need and strength areas, but less information about specific students. Lexile levels (B), when available, help identify texts at suitable reading levels for each student rather than inform instructional differentiation. Small-group projects (C) yield group, not individual, student results.

61. B: Literal comprehension is an understanding of what is actually stated in the text by the author. Questions of this type involve recalling information and often answer who, what, when, where, or why. Affective comprehension refers to readers' personal reactions to texts based on their individual experiences, prior knowledge, and preferences. Inferential comprehension is a deeper level of comprehension than literal comprehension. It requires readers to make inferences when the answers to questions are not directly stated in the text. Evaluative comprehension is a deeper level than both literal and inferential comprehension. It involves using prior knowledge and textual evidence to form judgments about the text.

62. C: Effective writing instruction not only teaches writing for its own sake, but also uses writing to improve reading comprehension and learning across the curriculum. It differentiates instruction via multiple tiers (A), which addresses individual student differences; teaches writing strategies explicitly (B), which enables students to understand and apply them; and provides authentic activities (D) and strategies to enhance student self-efficacy for writing, which increases student motivation to write.

63. C: Setting clear goals, observing concrete data, and applying learning are all aspects of inquiry strategies, so choice C is correct. Each of the other choices refers to a teaching approach or set of strategies that does not involve these elements. Prewriting strategies (A) include helping students generate ideas, organize ideas, access their background knowledge, identify research topics, and use graphics to visualize ideas. Modeling strategies (B) includes teacher demonstration, giving students exemplary models of expected writing types, helping students analyze models, and inviting students to emulate effective model elements in their writing. Process writing (D) includes giving students opportunities for extended practice, peer interaction, personal responsibility, writing for authentic audiences, and self-evaluation.

64. A: The teacher can best use this data to evaluate what topics and themes her students in general are having trouble learning. By utilizing this data from the clickers, it should be relatively easy for the teacher to see the common questions that were missed, which allows for the opportunity to reteach certain concepts. The benefits of using technology like this allow for information to be gathered and analyzed quicker than standard quizzing methods in a classroom.

65. B: Among the answer choices provided, the best option for helping students pronounce new words is to encourage students to sound out the words slowly, keeping the rules of vowels and consonants in mind. This is not, of course, the only option for assisting students with word pronunciation, but it is the best option among the available choices for this question.

66. A: Studies evaluating instructional methods for language and vocabulary learning have found that adding multimedia applications to enhance read-alouds and other instruction with grades pre-K through 2 reduces learning gaps between ELL and other students. However, learning enhancement from adding multimedia was statistically significant for ELLs only, not other students (B). Researchers find children have more difficulty recalling new word pronunciations than meanings, not vice versa (C). They also find that, when teachers add questions and comments about word meanings, children more likely learn those meanings (D).

67. C: In inclusive educational programs, teachers must be willing to find solutions to their own needs through team-based problem-solving, so choice C is correct. Teachers must also meet not only student needs but the needs of students' families, so choice A is incorrect. Additionally, teachers should effectively communicate their own needs, so choice B is incorrect. They should meet these needs through team problem-solving, as mentioned in choice C, and not by seeking solutions independently, so choice D is incorrect.

68. C: The main role of literature, as described in the passage, is to reflect societal issues and human experiences. The passage discusses how literature serves as a mirror to society, shedding light on issues such as racial injustice and totalitarianism. It emphasizes that literary works like *To Kill a Mockingbird* and *1984* provide valuable insights into the human condition by addressing and reflecting upon these societal issues and human experiences. While literature can certainly entertain and provide glimpses into historical events, the primary focus in this passage is on its role as a reflection of broader societal and human concerns.

69. B: "Pretty as a picture" is a simile, which is a comparison of two unlike things using the words *like* or *as*. A metaphor is a similar comparison between two unlike things, but metaphors do not use the words *like* or *as*. Synecdoche is a phrase that uses a part to represent the whole of something. For instance, one might refer to "the crown" to refer to a royal family. Finally, a paradox is a statement that appears to contradict itself. All of these are considered figures of speech.

70. B: Integrated curriculum is vital to student growth and to fostering a love of learning. In reality, all subject areas are related, and a good teacher will find ways to highlight the connection of concepts across the curriculum. In choice B, the science teacher provides a way to help students study for a test. However, she would probably be better advised to work with the students on comprehension and retention before test time arrives. She could use a variety of previewing and reviewing skills, as well as creative ways to bring the information to life during class discussions and activities. This teacher might also benefit from discussing the situation with a language arts teacher to get ideas on how to build skills in reading for information, main ideas, and supporting concepts.

71. C: Expository essays are any type of essay in which the writer is providing meaningful information about a topic for the purpose of informing. Most of the topics listed in the example include informational tasks, explaining the process of doing something, such as baking or juggling. Expository essays can use various organizational schemes to help structure the information, such as by comparing and contrasting two things. An expository essay is different from an argumentative essay in that it is not trying to convince the reader of anything, but only trying to inform. Similarly, the purpose of a descriptive essay is to show detail, but not necessarily to inform about how something works.

72. B: English language learners (ELLs) generally benefit from contextual learning of vocabulary because it helps to solidify the meaning and usage of the newly-learned words. Both vocabulary in isolation (a) and vocabulary in volume (b) typically refer to rote memorization, which does not provide the retention benefits or provide the student with contextual experience. Answer (d) is wrong because speech proficiency levels do not necessarily correspond to a student's reading and vocabulary skills.

73. D: Children's literature is not meant to instruct students in sciences, such as mathematics and biology; textbooks have that goal. Children's literature is designed to enhance moral values, instruct through entertaining stories, and promote a life-long interest in reading.

74. B: Language load is the number of unrecognizable words an English language learner encounters when reading a passage or listening to a teacher. Language load is one of the barriers English language learners face. To lighten this load, a teacher can rephrase, eliminate unnecessary words, divide complex sentences into smaller units, and teach essential vocabulary before the student begins the lesson.

75. D: Research finds that most teachers can plan differentiated instruction based on the findings of studies, and that they do this better when using individual scores of real students than with invented scores of hypothetical students. Research has found that teachers make data-based instructional decisions better in small groups than individually, not vice versa. Studies show that most teachers can locate data in graphs or tables, but have more trouble with data comprehension than vice versa. Research also finds that the majority of teachers have difficulty with both interpreting relationships among variables and posing questions.

76. B: Shakespeare (1564-1616) wrote during the Renaissance (B), which is generally considered to encompass the 15th and 16th centuries. The medieval (A) era, also known as the Middle Ages, was earlier, ending in the late 15th century, and included authors like Geoffrey Chaucer, Dante Alighieri, the author of *Sir Gawain and the Green Knight,* and Sir Thomas Malory. The Restoration (C) period in English literature followed the Renaissance, starting in the middle of the 17th century and ending before the 18th century. It included authors like John Dryden, who wrote poetry, satire, and criticism. The Enlightenment (D) occurred in the 18th century and included the authors Jonathan Swift, Alexander Pope, Dr. Samuel Johnson, and James Boswell.

77. C: The word *literature* has multiple meanings. A general meaning is all the written works in a given language, such as English literature. It can also mean the profession of a writer or author. Literature is also used to mean any kind of printed materials, like a company's promotional or informational literature, including pamphlets, brochures, and the like. However, in research fields, literature typically means all the research previously published on a given subject, such as research on self-correction in the psychology field of applied behavior analysis or on instructional strategies in the English language arts field of writing instruction.

78. C: Chopin's character development of Mrs. Mallard in the quotation includes repression and strength. These explain her not showing shock or denial but weeping immediately on hearing of her husband's apparent death, but also its short duration: "When the storm of grief had spent itself she went away to her room alone." The quotation does not explain her reaction to seeing her husband alive: identification of Louise's "heart trouble" in the first sentence helps explain her heart attack, along with character development indicating her relief at freedom from her husband's domination (despite his always loving her and her "sometimes" loving him). It does not explain his behavior: the paragraph describing his "powerful will bending hers" explains his controlling nature. The "joy" Chopin describes is NOT at seeing her husband alive, which kills her; Louise felt this joy previously upon believing he was dead ("free, free, free!").

79. B: Reading fluency refers to the speed, inflection and accuracy with which students read, either orally or silently. In order to read fluently, students must be able to decode, or break down into segments, words that adhere to the common rules of the English alphabet. For those words that are generally not easily decoded, students must build their vocabulary of "sight words," which should be recognized without the need to decode. In (A), students may or may not be reading fluently or accurately, since the computer program does not monitor how the student reads. In (C), keyboarding practice bears no direct relationship to reading fluency. In (D), again, the computer is simply a source for text, but does not build any specific fluency skill. In (B), students are exposed to sight words and vocabulary in a fun way. Using a computer program allows for an unlimited supply of relevant words and for accurate scoring.

80. C: The titles are in chronological order. A is incorrect because the titles do not show comparison and contrast. B is incorrect because the titles do not show cause and effect. D is incorrect because the titles do not show problem and solution.

81. A: This brief paragraph will encourage students to use writing as a means for personal exploration and self-expression. B is incorrect because this writing assignment is not a mandate to disagree with others. C is incorrect because the structure of the novel is not shown in the passage. D is incorrect because the plot of the novel is not shown in the passage.

82. B: Comprehension is a process of creating meaning from that which a student reads, sees, hears, or experiences. The tools for comprehending are similar across genres. The teacher has specifically chosen a passage and wants the students to compare, not contrast, the pieces. Dickensian writing is not generally considered to be journalistic, as suggested in Choice "a". Choice "c" is correct—you can in fact compare even unlike things. However, Choice "b" provides a richer backdrop for showing students how to link that which they read in school to their own lives and use the same tools to comprehend and take meaning from whatever they read.

83. C: All private and public schools will provide some sort of curriculum guidance, which usually takes the form of a list of concepts that must be covered within a certain time frame. Teachers must use this provision as a guideline for planning instruction. However, with time and creativity, teachers can bring these concepts to life using various types of material (e.g., oral, written, media, and performance) and engaging instructional methods. Teachers can also find ways to integrate instruction and concepts with teachers of other subjects to ensure that students understand that language skills are not only interrelated, but also applicable to all areas of learning.

84. C: In the process writing approach, elements include having students write for authentic audiences (A), interact with other students throughout the writing process (B), take personal responsibility for their written work (C), and self-evaluate their writing (D).

85. D: Expectations include interpreting and understanding visual imagery, meanings, and messages; analyzing and critiquing the importance of visual media; and evaluating the ways that various media inform and influence people. Developing and organizing ideas from the environment is an expectation, but not from the English Language Arts subject area; it is an expectation for middle school students in the Fine Arts subject area.

86. A: Experts do advise communications presenters to combine two or three types of media for the most effectiveness, rather than limiting themselves to only one (B). The presenter's budget will also necessarily influence their choice of media (C). For example, TV is more expensive than radio; radio is more expensive than paying a PR writer for print communications; and some presenters can produce their own news releases and photos at no additional cost. How long a communication is will affect the media choice (D), e.g., in terms of costs and of maintaining audience attention.

87. A: Using one paragraph to introduce one main point is advised, present evidence supporting that point, and explain how this point relates to the thesis. Each additional main point, its supporting evidence, and its relation to the thesis should occupy a separate paragraph. This method is summarized in choice A. Choice B is incorrect because main points should not be separated from their supporting evidence or the explanations of how they relate to the thesis. Choice C is incorrect because including all main points, their accompanying evidence, and their relation to the thesis in one long paragraph would provide almost no structure, making the essay more difficult to read and understand. Similarly, dividing topics into as many paragraphs as necessary, as is described in Choice D, can lead to an unnecessarily long and unfocused essay.

88. C: According to experts, research shows that teachers should explicitly teach their students writing strategies, including prewriting planning, composition, revision, and editing, by first modeling the strategies; then guiding students in practicing them; and then, once they have learned the strategies, letting students practice using them independently. They should not skip the guided practice step (A); students need assistance learning to apply demonstrated strategies before practicing on their own. Students learn better with, not without, teacher models (B), which must be presented before, not after, guided practice (D).

89. B: When teachers assign cooperative writing partnerships, each student in a pair should not always take only one role (A); they must both take turns writing and reviewing their partner's writing (B) to experience both roles in the process. Each student should provide not only positive feedback (C) or only constructive feedback (D) to a partner, but both. For example, if the assignment is using descriptive adjectives, positive feedback would be identifying specific descriptive adjectives the partner used; constructive feedback could be identifying sentences that could use more descriptive adjectives.

90. A: Cognates are words in different languages that share the same roots, such as the English word *conflict* and the Spanish word *conflicto*. If students know the meanings of the words in their native languages, they can apply that knowledge to determine the meanings of the English words. Realia are everyday objects that provide visual representations of words, also contributing to vocabulary development. While recognizing known parts in cognates can assist students with decoding new words quickly, it is less likely to assist with prosody. Phonological and phonemic awareness have to do with identifying and manipulating sounds in words rather than identifying word meanings or related spelling patterns.

Practice Test #2

Refer to the following for question 1:

Use the following stanzas from Alfred, Lord Tennyson's "The Charge of the Light Brigade"

Half a league, half a league,
Half a league onward,
All in the valley of Death
Rode the six hundred.
"Forward, the Light Brigade!
Charge for the guns!" he said.
Into the valley of Death
Rode the six hundred.

"Forward, the Light Brigade!"
Was there a man dismayed?
Not though the soldier knew
Someone had blundered.
Theirs not to make reply,
Theirs not to reason why,
Theirs but to do and die.
Into the valley of Death
Rode the six hundred.

1. How do the form and word choice of lines 13–15 in the second stanza contribute to their meaning?

a. They reflect the complexity of the battle through their variety.
b. They reflect the men's heroic humility and honesty through their simplicity.
c. They reflect the treacherous nature of war through their irregularity.
d. They reflect the tedium of the soldier's life through their monotony.

2. Which of the following practices would assist students in constructing meaning from a fictional text written long before the students were born?

a. After the text is read for homework, students discuss any aspects of the story that they did not understand or that were unfamiliar to them.
b. Students individually visualize scenery and events in the text as they read.
c. The class makes a list of unfamiliar words in the text and looks them up in the dictionary as the text is read.
d. Before the text is assigned, students learn about pertinent historical events or aspects of culture that informed the writing of the text.

3. For making speeches, which nonverbal behaviors enhance audience perceptions of speaker credibility?

a. Making eye contact with certain listeners
b. Making random/unrelated body motions
c. Making startling/novel facial expressions
d. Making gestures congruent with meaning

4. Of the following, which represents an indirect way in which students receive instruction in and learn vocabulary?

a. Being exposed repeatedly to vocabulary in multiple teaching contexts
b. Being exposed to vocabulary when adults read aloud to them
c. Being pre-taught specific words found in text prior to reading
d. Being taught vocabulary words over extended periods of time

5. What is an accurate reflection of criteria for clear, concise speech presentations?

a. A speaker should not take three or more minutes more to get to the point.
b. A speaker should not pause before answering audience questions.
c. A speaker should include as many anecdotes and details as possible.
d. A speaker should include both necessary and interesting information.

6. Among these literary genres, in which pair has one *most* been used within the other?

a. Nonfiction prose within poetry
b. Fictional prose within drama
c. Poetry within fictional drama
d. Poetry within nonfiction prose

7. What is the best way that a teacher can utilize the data from standardized tests from the previous year?

a. Seat students with similar deficiencies together in class to make it easier to facilitate learning
b. Identify the highest and the lowest achievers and enact a plan for the highest achievers to assist the lowest achievers
c. Identify the achievement gaps of each student and create a plan that addresses the largest gaps
d. Compare data with other teachers in the grade level to evaluate the best methods for instruction

8. In differentiated instruction classrooms, which is the most common type of differentiation?

a. The way individual students access content
b. The way that learning goals are assessed
c. The concepts individual students are taught
d. The amount of detail in teaching concepts

9. What do research studies find about student collaboration relative to effective writing instruction?

a. Cooperative learning does not apply to teaching writing.
b. Cooperative learning is an effective practice for writing.
c. Cooperative learning needs no structure from teachers.
d. Cooperative learning needs structure, not expectations.

10. As a reading comprehension aid, which type of graphic organizer would help students differentiate between fiction and nonfiction text structures?

a. Venn diagram
b. Storyboard
c. Story map
d. T-Chart

11. Which statement about the relationship between conflict and plot is most accurate?

a. Conflict is what drives the plot of a story forward.
b. Resolving the main conflict is often not the protagonist's primary endeavor.
c. Emotional, mental, and moral conflicts impact plot less than physical conflicts do.
d. The climax of a plot only occurs after the main conflict has resolved.

12. For which of the following purposes would a teacher use a formative assessment?

a. To get data to inform a school improvement plan
b. To get or keep government funding for the school
c. To get data about individual student performance
d. To get data on student progress over a school year

13. In character development analysis, which of the following is NOT likely to be helpful?

a. Paying attention to observations the narrator makes about a character
b. Observing apparent contradictions in a character's thoughts and behavior
c. Determining how a character could be used differently by the author
d. Noting how the narrator and the other characters speak differently about a character

14. In explanatory writing, which of the following does the writer typically NOT do?

a. Differentiate among the members of a given category
b. Assume some information is factual, accurate, or true
c. Prove certain information is factual, accurate and true
d. Define terms, analyze processes, or develop concepts

15. A teacher wants to help his students identify the types of nonfiction texts they are reading based on their text structures. Which keywords would students likely find in compare-and-contrast texts?

a. For example and for instance
b. Similarly and on the other hand
c. Because and as a result
d. First, next, and finally

16. Which author is associated with the Contemporary movement?

a. Homer
b. Henry David Thoreau
c. George Orwell
d. William Shakespeare

17. Concerning student self-monitoring strategies in reading, which statement is true?

a. If students do not comprehend something, they should identify what and locate it in the text.
b. Students should only employ self-monitoring techniques when working with texts they understand well.
c. Self-monitoring is generally considered ineffective for students who struggle with reading.
d. If students do not comprehend something, previewing text by looking ahead makes it worse.

18. When evaluating writing strategies, what does research find about effective instruction of middle school students?

a. Explicit instruction is best for teaching specific tasks, such as writing argumentative essays.
b. Explicit instruction is better for teaching brainstorming, editing, or other general processes.
c. Explicit instruction is necessary to teach specific, general, planning, and compositional tasks.
d. Explicit instruction is more important to teach revising and editing than planning for writing.

19. Which of the following strategies would most effectively work to meet the multiple learning needs of diverse students?

a. Enforcing a rigid schedule
b. Simplifying content for the whole class
c. Implementing a variety of different instructional daily activities
d. Incorporating more learning games to increase enthusiasm

20. Of the following statements, which is true about the relationship of reading fluency, word decoding, and reading comprehension?

a. Developing fluency in reading has no relationship to speed and automaticity with decoding words.
b. Students should have strong word recognition foundations established before fluency instruction.
c. Reading fluency shows faster information processing speed, but has no impact on comprehension.
d. Slower, less automatic word decoding decreases reading fluency, but it increases comprehension.

21. Silent reading fluency can best be assessed by:

a. Having the student retell or summarize the material to determine how much was understood.
b. Giving a written test that covers plot, theme, character development, sequence of events, rising action, climax, falling action, and outcome. A student must test at a 95% accuracy rate to be considered fluent at silent reading.
c. Giving a three-minute Test of Silent Contextual Reading Fluency four times a year. The student is presented with text in which spaces between words and all punctuation have been removed. The student must divide one word from another with slash marks, as in the example: The/little/sailboat/bobbed/so/far/in/the/distance/it/looked/like/a/toy. The more words a student accurately separates, the higher the silent reading fluency score.
d. Silent reading fluency cannot be assessed. It is a private act between the reader and the text and does not invite critique.

22. Which of these elements is LESS likely to be found in drama than in other genres of literature?

a. Characters
b. Narrative
c. Conflict
d. Action

23. Young children tend to learn vocabulary more effectively when under certain levels of demand. Which of the following best represents an appropriate use of demand for activities made to support acquisition of new vocabulary words?

a. Teachers alternate between low-demand and high-demand questions.
b. Teachers employ new vocabulary in clear contexts, but do not provide direct support.
c. Teachers restrict their questions to those with low complexity until students demonstrate mastery.
d. Teachers move from low-demand question to high-demand ones.

24. Among effective reading strategies, which one involves recalling relevant past experience and existing knowledge to construct meaning from the new information in text that one reads?

a. Inferring
b. Activating
c. Questioning
d. Summarizing

25. Two mothers of young children write their observations about parenting. Writer A publishes her writing daily for a wide reading audience. Writer B also writes daily, but privately. Which two forms of writing best identify their activities?

a. Blog; journal
b. Journal; letters
c. Letters; essays
d. Essays; speeches

26. Among these procedural devices that help students plan and revise writing, which is helpful as an aid for remembering key sets of information?

a. Outlines
b. Checklists
c. Mnemonic devices
d. Graphic organizers

27. *Beowulf* is an epic poem that is important because it is often viewed as the first significant work of English literature. Although it was first written in AD 700, it is thought to be even hundreds of years older than that. It is believed that the story of *Beowulf* was told for centuries before it ever made its way on to paper. It is still taught today in various schools and universities.

***Beowulf* is a significant poem because:**

a. It was first written down in AD 700.
b. It was told for centuries before it was written down.
c. It is still taught today in academic settings.
d. It is the first important work of English literature.

28. Which assessment will determine a student's ability to identify initial, medial, blended, final, segmented, and manipulated "units"?

a. Phonological awareness assessment
b. High-frequency word assessment
c. Reading fluency assessment
d. Comprehension quick-check

29. Ms. Benson has scheduled a family conference to discuss a student's academic progress. The family is from another country, and although they speak English, Ms. Benson is worried that cultural differences may lead to cross-cultural misunderstanding. Which of the following should she be mindful of to avoid this situation?

a. Protecting her student's right to confidentiality
b. Ensuring she is prepared with documentation of the student's academic progress
c. Using appropriate verbal and nonverbal communication
d. Keeping the conference informational and focusing on the student's strengths

30. Which of the following is true about how teachers should use formal and informal instruments for formative assessment in the classroom?

a. Teachers should use multiple formal and informal assessments as bases for student grouping.
b. Teachers should use only formal test instruments for conducting their formative assessments.
c. Teachers should select one specific formal or informal assessment instrument to use exclusively.
d. Teachers should use formative assessments only for evaluating students, not for teaching them.

31. The term *soliloquy* is used to refer to an element typically found in which literary genre/subgenre?

a. Drama
b. Poetry
c. Novels
d. Essays

Refer to the following for question 32:

> Jo's face was a study next day, for the secret rather weighed upon her, and she found it hard not to look mysterious and important. Meg observed it, but did not trouble herself to make inquiries, for she had learned that the best way to manage Jo was by the law of contraries, so she felt sure of being told everything if she did not ask. She was rather surprised, therefore, when the silence remained unbroken, and Jo assumed a patronizing air, which decidedly aggravated Meg, who in turn assumed an air of dignified reserve and devoted herself to her mother. This left Jo to her own devices, for Mrs. March had taken her place as nurse, and bade her rest, exercise, and amuse herself after her long confinement. Amy being gone, Laurie was her only refuge, and much as she enjoyed his society, she rather dreaded him just then, for he was an incorrigible tease, and she feared he would coax the secret from her.
>
> (*Little Women* by Louisa May Alcott)

32. From what point of view is this passage written?

a. First person
b. Second person
c. Third person
d. Fourth person

33. The Cognitive Academic Language Learning Approach (CALLA) is found to be helpful for middle school ELL students. What is true of this approach?

a. It includes content objectives but does not include language objectives.
b. It includes language objectives but does not include content objectives.
c. It has content and language objectives, but there are none for learning strategies.
d. It allows thematically based content or formats using sheltered content.

34. A teacher wants to help her students develop metacognitive skills. Which guiding question can she prompt students to ask themselves while reading?

a. Who are the major and minor characters?
b. Were my predictions correct?
c. What happened first?
d. What is the theme of the story?

35. Providing a learning assignment wherein a student is engaged in hands-on activities like manipulating objects, participating in sports, or dancing would appeal most to which of Gardner's multiple intelligences?

a. Intrapersonal
b. Bodily-Kinesthetic
c. Naturalist
d. Visual-Spatial

36. With a teacher's guidance, a class brainstorms main ideas, topics, or concepts from a text. Students choose a select number of these ideas and copy them onto separate index cards. The students then individually review the text, recording any supporting evidence on the notecard with the applicable main idea. This activity would be an excellent pre-lesson for teaching which skill set?

a. Working as a group to interpret a text and write an appropriate and realistic sequel, focusing on interpretive comprehension and creative writing
b. Silent reading as a form of comprehension practice
c. Organizing ideas for writing a cohesive and persuasive essay or research paper that asserts supported arguments with valid supporting evidence
d. Literal and figurative comprehension, as well as contributing to group discussions via oral communication skills

37. Jamie's teacher presents her class with a unit about Mexico that includes information about the customs, geography, language, and cuisine of the country. While the teacher is showing pictures of a traditional Mexican festival, Jamie raises his hand to share some of the object-names he remembers from his family's annual trip to Mexico. This scenario is an example of:

a. Paradigm emergence
b. Prior knowledge activation
c. Chunking
d. Immersion theory

38. Which of the following best describes the effect of initiating and maintaining effective communication with students' families on student development and achievement?

a. Students' families will have access to weekly progress reports regarding their children's grades.
b. Students' families will feel welcomed and encouraged to participate in their children's education program.
c. The teacher will be able to establish a more culturally responsive learning environment.
d. Students' attendance rates will improve, fostering greater academic achievement.

39. Which of these is more characteristic of a summative assessment?

a. The teacher administers it frequently during instruction.
b. The teacher uses its results to inform teaching changes.
c. The teacher gives it after lessons, units, or school years are complete.
d. The teacher relies on it for individualizing student data.

40. Which instructional activity is the best example of the research-based strategy of activating students' prior knowledge before reading?

a. Before students read a text, the teacher instructs them in relevant background information.
b. Before and after they read a text, the teacher has students make a KWL chart on its subject.
c. After students have read a text, the teacher asks them what they know about the subject.
d. The teacher asks students to express their opinions and reactions on a topic after reading.

41. A writing assignment asks the student to do things like organize, plan, formulate, assemble, compose, construct, or arrange some material they have read or learned. Which of the following cognitive (learning) objectives is the teacher aiming to meet with this assignment?

a. Analysis
b. Synthesis
c. Evaluation
d. Application

42. Which of these components of speech delivery is most effective for establishing rapport and personal connection with the audience?

a. Eye contact
b. Vocal tones
c. Articulation
d. Movement

43. Making a strong argument in a speech, conversation, or debate requires:

a. Forceful delivery
b. Acknowledging the opposing point of view with respect
c. Demonstrating the weakness of the opposing view with mockery
d. Seizing the floor when the opponent's point is strong
e. Seizing the floor when the opponent's point is weak

44. Relative to formative and summative assessments, research reveals that the single greatest change in classroom instruction for improving student learning and achievement is effective _____, which students and teachers get best from _____ assessments.

a. comparison; summative
b. feedback; formative
c. feedback; summative
d. comparison; formative

45. Which of the following literary theories would most inform Conrad's *Heart of Darkness*?

a. Aristotle's theory of unity
b. Feminist and gender theories
c. Post-colonial theories
d. Marxist theories

46. Which of these correctly represents findings about research-based vocabulary instruction?

a. Children need word repetition consisting of drills for vocabulary development.
b. Children need only be exposed to new words once or twice to remember them.
c. Children learn the vocabulary in texts best indirectly through simply reading them.
d. Children require direct instruction and word exposure in various contexts.

47. Before Charles Darwin published *On the Origin of Species,* which of the following historical developments reflected resistance to ideas of evolution like his?

a. Georges Buffon's earlier suggestions concerning potentially common ancestries of similar species
b. Georges Cuvier's established proof of extinction from comparing fossils and contemporary bones
c. Carl Linnaeus's classification and John Ray's taxonomy viewing species as divinely designed and unchanging
d. Jean-Baptiste Lamarck's theory of environmental adaptation, heredity, and increasing complexity

48. A teacher reads to her students at least once a week. This month, she plans to read poetry to her class. The students will then discuss what they have heard for the rest of each class period. What is this teacher's most likely purpose in designing these lessons?

a. To give students a break from extensive reading requirements.
b. To build phonological awareness, specifically of rhyming words.
c. To teach students that there is more to literature than prose.
d. To increase students' listening skills while exposing them to new kinds of literature.

49. A teacher gives students a list of words, including *care*, *home*, and *use*, and asks them to record the definitions. Next, she asks them to add *less* to the ends of the words and record the new definitions. Students are then instructed to write down their observations in their writing journals. What is the primary purpose of this activity?

a. Helping students recognize the meaning of a common suffix
b. Teaching students the *-less* spelling pattern
c. Practicing word analysis skills that will assist with decoding
d. Identifying commonly used prefixes

50. According to the ancient Classical definitions, also used by Shakespeare and other playwrights, which of these is NOT necessarily true of the drama subgenres of comedy and tragedy?

a. Comedy is humorous, and it makes audiences laugh.
b. Comedy may not be funny, but it has a happy ending.
c. Tragedy ends in sadness, and it often involves death.
d. Tragedy inspires terror and pity from the audience.

51. A school has always had a no hat or headwear rule in its dress code policy. Recently, an immigrant from Iran who wears religious head garb enrolled in the school. The school allowed for her to wear something on her head as an exception to the policy but still maintained no headwear in other situations. What effect does this MOST likely have for the student?

a. The student will feel special and unique because she is allowed to wear religious head garb.
b. The student may feel different and singled out, creating an environment in the school that is not accepting of differences.
c. The student will be indifferent to this because at least she is able to wear her head garb.
d. The student may feel it is unfair toward other students that they also cannot wear anything on their heads and begin protesting.

52. A struggling reader has difficulty comprehending vocabulary words when they are encountered in unfamiliar texts. She frequently uses a dictionary to look up the unknown words. While this helps her figure out the meanings of the words, it interrupts her fluency and affects comprehension. Her teacher, Mr. Palmer, would like to teach her other strategies she can use instead that will minimize the disruptions to her fluency and increase her comprehension. Which strategy would likely be most effective?

a. Quickly asking a classmate for the meanings of the words
b. Creating a list of the unknown words and looking them up later
c. Trying to determine the meanings of the words from context clues
d. Skipping over the words she does not know as long as the sentences make sense

53. What advice to teachers does research indicate about writing instruction strategies?

a. Explicitly instruct sentence combining to develop sophisticated sentences.
b. Computer word-processing is a crutch that defeats student independence.
c. A process writing approach is incompatible with research-based strategies.
d. Help students analyze writing models, but do not let them imitate models.

54. A cloze test evaluates a student's:

a. Reading fluency
b. Understanding of context and vocabulary
c. Phonemic skills
d. Ability to apply the alphabetic principle to previously unknown material

55. Which type of nonverbal message deals with belonging, control, respect, or disapproval?

a. Emotive messages
b. Relational messages
c. Relationship messages
d. Interpersonal messages

56. Among the following instructional activities, which one is *more* likely to develop critical listening skills for evaluating the message communicated than to develop listening skills for appreciating and enjoying spoken language?

a. Listening to the novel *Charlotte's Web* (White, 1952) read aloud for a class of K-1-age students
b. Listening to the poem *The Bells* by Edgar Allan Poe (1849) in either a live reading or recording
c. Listening to an actor's live or recorded reading of Lewis Carroll's *Jabberwocky* (1871)
d. Listening to a live or recorded radio commercial advertising a new product's miraculous benefits

57. Which choice describes the most complete method of displaying student achievement or progress in language arts?

a. A written report or story that demonstrates a student's knowledge of grammar, spelling, comprehension, and writing skills.
b. Either a norm- or criterion-referenced test that breaks language skills into small subsets and provides achievement levels for each skill.
c. A portfolio containing a log of stories or books the student has read, rates of reading fluency, writing samples, creative projects, and spelling, grammar, and comprehension tests/quizzes.
d. A year-end project in which the student presents what he or she has learned from a student-chosen book; the student must read an excerpt of the story and display a visual aid highlighting important information from the story or literary techniques used by the author.

58. Which of the following is the best use of technology in a language arts classroom?

a. Providing laptops to students to achieve more effective note-taking, access to word processing programs, and access to the internet
b. Encouraging the use of slide shows or similar programs to support lectures and oral presentations, as well as to organize pertinent class concepts
c. Incorporating a computer-based "language lab" in which students can listen to texts and engage in interactive word-study and comprehension activities
d. Whenever possible, watching film interpretations based on texts studied in class

59. Which student is most likely to need referral to a reading specialist for assessment, special instruction, or intervention?

a. Annabel: a second-grade student who tends to skip over words or phrases when she reads, affecting her comprehension of the text.
b. Cliff: a kindergarten student who is already reading simple chapter books with his parents at home or in class.
c. Noelle: a first grader who avoids any activity in which she must read, both aloud or silently, preferring to ask an adult to read the text for her first.
d. Barrett: a third grader who often confuses the sounds of certain letters, such as /b/ and /d/ or /v/ and /u/.

60. When teachers assign students to small groups for collaborative writing, which of these applies?

a. Teachers should only set individual performance expectations for individual, not group work.
b. Teachers should expect student groups to self-manage, and not interfere by giving structure.
c. Classmates in collaborative groups should give each other positive feedback, not corrections.
d. Classmates in collaborative groups should give each other constructive and positive feedback.

61. Which pair contains terms typically applied to two subgenres of *two different* literary genres, rather than to two subgenres of the *same single* literary genre?

a. Picaresque and epistolary
b. Historical and speculative
c. Persuasive and expository
d. Bildungsroman and elegy

62. Collaborative Strategic Reading (CSR) is a teaching technique that depends on two teaching practices. These practices are:

a. Cooperative learning and reading comprehension
b. Cooperative reading and metacognition
c. Reading comprehension and metacognition
d. Cooperative learning and metacognition

63. Of the following examples, which one is NOT an open-ended question?

a. "When does the climax of this story occur?"
b. "Is this expression a simile or a metaphor?"
c. "How are similes and metaphors different?"
d. "What are some reasons we have poetry?"

Refer to the following for questions 64–65:

There Will Come Soft Rains

By Sara Teasdale

There will come soft rains and the smell of the ground,
And swallows circling with their shimmering sound;

And frogs in the pools singing at night,
And wild plum trees in tremulous white;

Robins will wear their feathery fire
Whistling their whims on a low fence-wire;

And not one will know of the war, not one
Will care at last when it is done.

Not one would mind, neither bird nor tree
If mankind perished utterly;

And Spring herself, when she woke at dawn,
Would scarcely know that we were gone.

64. How many stanzas does this poem have?

a. 2
b. 4
c. 6
d. 12

65. The *we* used in the final line ("Would scarcely know that we were gone") refers to:

a. All of mankind
b. The victors of the war
c. Americans
d. The poet and the reader

66. Which of the following is true?

a. a simile compares different things by using a word such as like or as.
b. a metaphor compares different things by using a word such as like or as.
c. a metaphor makes a comparison while a simile does not.
d. a simile makes a comparison while a metaphor does not.

67. A classroom teacher observes that a new ELL student consistently omits the /h/ sound in words. Of these, what is the first factor the teacher should consider?

a. The student may have an articulation disorder.
b. The student may be a native Spanish speaker.
c. The student may need a hearing assessment.
d. The student may have a respiratory problem.

68. Paragraphs usually function in one of six major roles: introduction, definition, illustration, information, transition, and conclusion. How would the teacher describe a transitional paragraph to her students for their writing purposes?

a. It engages the reader and prepares for the reading ahead.
b. It provides definitions for information.
c. It progresses from one aspect of the subject to another.
d. It presents examples to clarify the author's ideas.

Refer to the following for question 69:

A class considers the paragraph below:

Sarah and Kelly grinned at one another conspiratorially as they approached Dad, who was quietly reading his paper in the living room. "Dad, we'd like to ride our bikes down to Emil's house today," giggled Kelly. She glanced at her sister and shifted her weight from foot to foot. Dad appeared to think this over for a moment and replied, "Sure, that's fine with me!" The girls scampered to get their bikes and were soon on their way. With the children gone, Dad noticed how peaceful and quiet the house sounded. His reverie was quickly interrupted as he heard Mom calling from upstairs, "okay, everybody, I told you at breakfast that I need as much help as I can get to help me give the dog a bath, clean the house and finish the laundry today!" Dad groaned, knowing that he had been conned!

69. Which method would be best for helping students determine the meaning of the word "reverie" in the next to last sentence?

a. Using context clues
b. Making an educated guess
c. Decoding the prefix, root, and suffix of the word
d. Previewing and reviewing

70. On the first day of school, a teacher asks her students to create a list of tasks they feel they do well. What is the primary way in which this activity can help the teacher throughout the year?

a. It is a way for the teacher to informally assess her students' abilities and learn about their interests.
b. It serves as a tool the teacher can use to assess each student's background knowledge.
c. It will help the teacher know which students to pair in groups based on their skills.
d. It helps the students feel confident about what they already know.

71. Which of the following choices describes the best introduction to a unit on oral traditions from around the world?

a. Introducing games that practice new sight words, encoding words based on phonics rules, and answering short comprehension questions.
b. Setting up video-conferencing with a school in Asia so that students can communicate with children from other countries.
c. Inviting a guest speaker from a nearby Native American group to demonstrate oral storytelling to the class.
d. Creating a slide show presentation about various types of oral cultures and traditions and characteristics of each.

72. For supporting language acquisition in ESL/ELL students, what is most accurate about research-based instructional practices?

a. Teachers should only state directions verbally to give ELLs English decoding practice.
b. Teachers should encourage ESL students to respond rapidly to get them up to speed.
c. Teachers should use idioms without explanations to familiarize ELL students to these.
d. Teachers should give ELL students models and examples of what they expect in tasks.

73. Which of the following is true about the author's point of view in an informational text?

a. Readers can easily identify the author's point of view because informational texts include it as a main idea.
b. Readers often must infer the author's point of view because informational authors tend not to explicitly state it.
c. Readers may see the author's point of view equally well for neutral, balanced, and opinionated positions.
d. Readers who must analyze a text to identify the author's point of view can assume the text is poorly written.

74. Which strategy can be used to build readers' confidence and increase both comprehension and fluency when introducing an unknown text?

a. Introducing new vocabulary before reading
b. Reading the first few pages aloud before asking students to finish it independently
c. Listing what students want to learn about the topic
d. Asking students to predict what the text will be about based on the title and cover

75. A student learning English as a second language (ESL) who has limited comprehension of English and can speak one- to two-word English answers, essential English words, present-tense English verbs, and some familiar English phrases is in which stage of second-language acquisition?

a. Preproduction
b. Early Production
c. Speech Emergence
d. Intermediate Fluency

76. A teacher notices that her new student, Carl, has a hard time answering questions related to comprehension during class and has scored low on comprehension quizzes and worksheets. What would be the most logical first step in determining how to help Carl?

a. Encourage Carl to read all assigned texts at least twice before class to help him understand what he has read.
b. Provide Carl with story maps of what he will be reading to assist his comprehension visually.
c. Ask Carl to read aloud with his teacher individually so that she can ensure that he is reading with expected accuracy and speed (i.e., fluently).
d. Modify Carl's class work so that he is able to work on easier comprehension material until his skills are brought up to speed.

77. A teacher is instructing students in listening strategies for evaluating the effectiveness of the messages they hear. Which of the following strategies is a bottom-up strategy?

a. Listening to identify the main idea
b. Listening to identify specific details
c. Listening to summarize the content
d. Listening to infer or make predictions

78. In comparing and contrasting the sonnet and the ballad as subgenres of the literary genre of poetry, which of these do both forms have in common?

a. They both have five main kinds.
b. They both often express love.
c. They both began with music.
d. They both have equal meter.

79. Of the following statements, which is correct about formative and summative assessments?

a. Summative assessments help students meet learning standards-based goals on time.
b. Formative assessments allow teachers to adjust instruction to make it more effective.
c. Summative assessments typically involve students more in the assessment processes.
d. Formative assessments are more often used for accountability and calculating grades.

Refer to the following for question 80:

NOTE: The instructor of a history class has just finished grading the essay exams from his students, and the results are not good. The essay exam was worth 70% of the final course score. The highest score in the class was a low B, and more than half of the class of 65 students failed the exam. In view of this, the instructor reconsiders his grading plan for the semester and sends out an email message to all students.

Dear Students:

The scores for the essay exam have been posted in the online course grade book. By now, many of you have probably seen your grade and are a little concerned, since this accounts for 70% of your final grade. (And if you're not concerned, you should be—at least a bit!) At the beginning of the semester, I informed the class that I have a strict grading policy and that all scores will stand unquestioned. With each class comes a new challenge, however, and as any good instructor will tell you, sometimes the original plan has to change. As a result,

I propose the following options for students to make up their score:

1. I will present the class with an extra credit project at the next course meeting. The extra credit project will be worth 150% of the point value of the essay exam that has just been completed. While I will not drop the essay exam score, I will give you more than enough of a chance to make up the difference and raise your overall score.
2. I will allow each student to develop his or her own extra credit project. This project may reflect the tenor of option number 1 (above) but will allow the student to create a project more in his or her own line of interest. Bear in mind, however, that this is more of a risk. The scoring for option number 2 will be more subjective, depending on whether or not I feel that the project is a successful alternative to the essay exam. If it is, the student will be awarded up to 150% of the point value of the essay exam.

3. I will provide the class with the option of developing a group project. Students may form groups of 3 to 4 and put together an extra credit project that reflects a stronger response to the questions in the essay exam. This extra credit project will also be worth 150% of the point value of the essay exam. Note that each student will receive an equal score for the project, so there is a risk in this as well. If you are part of a group in which you do most of the work, each member of the group will receive equal credit for it. The purpose of the group project is to allow students to work together and arrive at a stronger response than if each worked individually.

If you are interested in pursuing extra credit to make up for the essay exam, please choose one of the options above. No other extra credit opportunities will be provided for the course.

Good luck!

Dr. Edwards

80. Which of the following describes this type of writing?

a. Technical
b. Narrative
c. Persuasive
d. Expository

81. Which statement best reflects factors that can interfere with diverse parents' and families' communication and participation in their children's education??

a. Language barriers rarely stop parents/families from communicating.
b. Parents with unsuccessful school histories try harder to participate.
c. Families can be alienated from school processes because of culture.
d. Poor past school experiences induce parents to help their children.

82. Which author was among the founders of the Modernist movement and authored *A Room of One's Own* in 1929?

a. Fyodor Dostoevsky
b. Francis Bacon
c. Charles Dickens
d. Virginia Woolf

83. Each week, a teacher asks one student to bring in a recording of his favorite song and a written version of the lyrics. The students listen to the song and receive a copy of the lyrics. They discuss these words as either one large group or in small groups. What are these students probably learning from this exercise?

a. Students are learning about the lives of their peers indirectly by listening to each student's favorite song; they can begin to understand each other by the meaning behind the song lyrics.
b. Students are learning that they are very diverse in many ways: they have different musical tastes and prefer many different styles of music and expression.
c. Students are learning that it is very difficult to communicate freely when bound by various musical traits such as rhyming, rhythm, and phrasing.
d. Students are learning that literacy skills do not just pertain to schoolwork. These skills allow students to understand and communicate meanings through a variety of ways, including music and lyrics.

84. Among multicultural factors for teachers to remember when interacting with students' parents, which is represented accurately?

a. Although facial expressions vary widely across cultures, personal space is identical universally.
b. Cultural and religious rules about casual physical contact differ very little across global nations.
c. Parents not forthcoming about their own education can be assumed lacking in this department.
d. Teachers should not assume that parents who dress humbly have lower socioeconomic levels.

85. A student encounters a multisyllabic word. She's not sure if she's seen it before. What should she do first? What should she do next?

a. Locate familiar word parts, then locate the consonants
b. Locate the consonants, then locate the vowels
c. Locate the vowels, then locate familiar word parts
d. Look it up in the dictionary, then write down the meaning

86. In the genre of poetry, which of the following is the term for a group of related ideas that is expressed in multiple lines of text and separated from other such groups by spaces?

a. Verse
b. Stanza
c. Refrain
d. Paragraph

87. "This treatise developed from an initial idea like a plant develops from a seed." The preceding sentence is an example of which literary device and argument method?

a. Analogy
b. Allegory
c. Allusion
d. Antithesis

88. Which of the following is most accurate about the relationship between the physics of thinking and speaking as these inform classroom instruction in listening actively?

a. Because thinking outpaces speech, students' minds wander, so listening is less effective than reading.
b. The disparity between speaking and thinking speeds is conducive to active listening via summarizing.
c. The process of listening is an inherently social interaction; the process of learning is not equally social.
d. The process of learning is essentially a reciprocal one, but the process of listening is not as reciprocal.

89. A teacher wants to work on her students' listening comprehension in addition to their reading comprehension since she understands that the skills are interrelated. She has a series of short stories that she thinks the students will enjoy. Which of the following would be the best supplement to typical written comprehension exercises?

a. Preview the content and then read the stories aloud to the students. Assess listening comprehension through verbal and written questions.
b. Ask the students to choose one story each to read aloud to a small group. Encourage the students to discuss what they have learned afterward.
c. Assign each student a story to read and require them to write a report on it. Each student should then present his or her report based on what he or she has learned to the class.
d. Have the students read stories aloud to the class, and create mock tests based upon the main ideas which they identify.

90. Mrs. Baines' sixth-grade class is preparing for their "World Community" project in which each student selects a famous person from another country to research and report upon. The student will compile research into a written report and create a poster with interesting pictures and visual images related to that person. The students will also deliver a speech or series of quotations originally spoken by their research subject. Why would Mrs. Baines include this last portion of the project?

a. To help her students get ready for the play they will put on later in the year, practicing speaking another person's words with expression and interest
b. To help students connect individual identity and oral expression while thinking about the world from another person's perspective
c. To provide material for the listening recall and comprehension portions of the unit quizzes and tests
d. To round out a project that is predominantly focused on reading and writing by adding a bit of speech into the requirements

Answer Key and Explanations for Test #2

1. B: These lines do not involve a lot of variety (A) but rather, contain very simple, short words—only two with two syllables, the rest with just one—as well as a consistent rhythm. Also, all three lines begin with the same word (*Theirs*), and all three end with rhyming words (*reply*, *why*, *die*). This simplicity reflects the meaning that the soldiers do not talk back to their superiors and do not conjecture about rationales for the battle, but simply do their jobs, which often includes dying. These lines are not irregular (C) in rhyme, meter, word choice, word length, etc. Though regular, they are not monotonous (D); in fact, they are some of the most famous, oft-quoted lines from the poem.

2. D: Teachers know that students are often expected to read works written long ago and whose relevance may not be immediately apparent. It is important that students have the information required to understand how the text was created. In Choice "d", students have the opportunity to learn about the socio-historical context in which the author created the piece. Armed with knowledge about the story's context, students can categorize and comprehend any of its aspects that would ordinarily be unclear. Students can also use this knowledge to find similarities and differences between aspects of their own lives and the context of the characters in the story. In choices "a" and "b," students are given the responsibility of determining what is important or unclear in the story. However, without understanding the work's context, students may not even be aware of the relevant information in the text, or may incorrectly interpret some events in the story. In Choice "c", the sole focus is on vocabulary, which may neglect other important characteristics of the writing.

3. D: Nonverbal behaviors during speeches influence the listeners' perceptions of the speaker's competence, good character, trustworthiness, and therefore credibility. Speakers should make eye contact with everybody in the audience, not just certain listeners (A). Their body movements should not be random or unrelated (B) to what they are saying (e.g., pacing, face rubbing, playing with one's hair, tapping pencils or toes, etc.), but they should reinforce their verbal messages. Facial expressions should not be startling or unexpected (C); they should be consistent with both the verbal content and the speaker's vocal tones. A speaker's gestures should also be congruent with the meaning (D) of what s/he is saying, to fit with and emphasize the points they are communicating.

4. B: Indirect ways in which students receive instruction and learn vocabulary include through daily conversations, reading on their own, and being read aloud to by adults. Direct instruction and learning in vocabulary include teachers providing extended instruction exposing students repeatedly to vocabulary words in multiple teaching contexts, teachers pre-teaching specific words found in text prior to students reading it, and teachers instructing students over extended time periods and having them actively work with vocabulary words.

5. A: When a speaker is making a statement or answering a question from the audience, s/he should not take three or more minutes to get to the point, which will lose listener attention. Getting off the subject has the same effect. However, speakers should not be afraid to pause before answering audience questions (B): this gives them time to formulate a clear response, as well as demonstrating to their listeners that they are thoughtful and in control. Including too many anecdotes and details (C) is not good: it causes audiences to lose track of the subject/get confused. Similarly, speakers should include necessary information but not all other interesting information.

(D): Information overload triggers listeners' brains to shut down due to having more input than they can process.

6. C: William Shakespeare's plays are good literary examples of poetry within fictional drama because they are written in verse form. Poems typically do not contain inserted prose (A). Plays are not generally known to incorporate pieces of fictional prose (B). Nonfictional prose sometimes incorporates quotations of poetry or even occasionally original poems, but this occurs much less often than with Shakespeare's plays and many others written entirely or mostly in poetry (D).

7. C: The best way that a teacher could use standardized test data in her classroom is to use it to analyze gaps in learning that her students may have. They could potentially identify common gaps among the students and identify which students struggled more on specific standards than other students. It allows for the teacher to have an opportunity to plan out what she wants her students to improve upon in the upcoming year and enact a plan to see them achieve.

8. A: In classrooms based on differentiated instruction, the most common differentiation is the way in which individual students access the content they learn, as individual student differences often dictate differential means of access. It is common for learning goals to be assessed by standardized testing, which is not differentiated as often except when individual students require alternative assessment. All students in the differentiated classroom should be taught the same concepts. The only differentiation is the level of complexity at which concepts are taught, which is individualized. Instructional concepts should not be detailed, but broad and generalized for all students to acquire the same principles and skills.

9. B: Studies show that cooperative learning is an effective practice for teaching many things, including writing (A). Experts recommend that when assigning cooperative writing partners or groups, teachers provide students with both a structure (C), and explicit expectations (D) for both partnership/group and individual performance.

10. C: A story map helps students identify text elements to chart text structure. This in turn helps them differentiate fiction vs. nonfiction, which have different text structures (e.g., nonfiction uses main idea and supporting details as elements; fiction uses setting, characters, plot, problems and solutions, etc.). A Venn diagram (A) helps students compare and contrast. A storyboard (B) helps students sequence text events and points. A T-Chart (D) helps students chart cause-and-effect, comparison-contrast, etc.

11. A: The plot of a story is a set of events, and each event is impacted by a conflict that a character in the story is experiencing. Thus, conflict drives the plot of the story forward, and there cannot be a plot without some kind of conflict. Choice B is incorrect because, in most stories, the protagonist's goal is to resolve the main conflict. In fact, for many protagonists, their personal goals or troubles contribute to or form the main conflict. Choice C is incorrect because the impact that each type of conflict has on the plot depends on the story. Choice D is incorrect because the main conflict is generally resolved in the climax of a plot, not before it.

12. C: To get data to inform a school improvement plan (a), a teacher could use a summative assessment, comparing student scores at the end of the school year to their baseline scores obtained at the beginning of that year. This can also be done to show accountability to the federal government (e.g., meeting adequate yearly progress criteria) to get or keep school funding (b); and to get data on student progress toward instructional objectives over the entire school year (d). A teacher would use a formative assessment to get data about individual student performance (c); summative assessments yield more group data and less individual data.

13. C: Among the choices, only choice C seems unlikely to be helpful in character analysis. In order to understand a literary character and analyze his or her development, readers should keep a few things in mind. One element to pay close attention to is the observations the narrator makes about a character, as the author likely has a reason for including these in the work (A). The reader can also observe contradictions in what a character thinks, says, and does, as these may reveal internal conflict and may play a role in the character's development (B). Additionally, readers can note differences between how the other characters in the story talk about a character and how the narrator talks about the character. This can reveal facts about the character's relationships with other characters, for example, and reveal how aware a character is of their own behavior or qualities.

14. C: Proving that something is factual, accurate, or true is typically what a writer of argumentative or persuasive writing does. Writers of explanatory writing, in contrast, will assume that something is factual, accurate, and true and then analyze, explain, and clarify this information to help readers understand it. This explanation can include differentiating among members of a given category; defining certain terms; analyzing or breaking down processes into their stages, phases, steps, or components; and/or developing concepts for the reading audience. Argumentative writing works to convince readers that something is so; explanatory writing works to explain why something is so.

15. B: The keywords in choice B are used to signal how two or more items are the same and different, which is the purpose of compare-and-contrast texts. The keywords in choice A would likely be found in descriptive texts. The keywords in choice C would likely be found in cause-and-effect texts. The keywords in choice D would likely be found in sequential texts.

16. C: Authors of the Contemporary movement wrote from 1945 to the present. George Orwell wrote *Animal Farm* in 1945 and *1984* in 1949.

17. A: One self-monitoring strategy to aid reading comprehension is for students to locate the problem by isolating what part of the text they do not understand, which words were difficult, and specifically what did not make sense to them. Another self-monitoring strategy for students is trying to paraphrase the text they had trouble understanding, which often helps. An additional strategy is to review the text for earlier instances of the same topic or information the student finds unclear to see if those shed light on the current instance. Another self-monitoring strategy is to preview the text to see if explanations, elaboration, illustrations or other graphics later in the text might clarify what students are currently reading. Self-monitoring techniques are important tools for those who struggle with reading, and they can be employed at all difficulty levels.

18. C: For teaching middle school students effective writing strategies, teachers need to give explicit instruction in specific tasks such as steps in writing argumentative essays (A) and in more general processes such as brainstorming, editing, etc. (B); teachers also should give explicit instruction in planning before writing and in revising and editing during writing (D). Explicit instruction is equally important to teach effective strategies for all of these.

19. C: When teachers use numerous types of instructional activities, they address multiple learning needs of students in their classroom. Not all students respond well to rigid schedules, so this would not appeal to a diverse class. Simplifying content for the whole class could negatively affect higher achieving students in the class and limit the potential for growth. While learning games could increase enthusiasm, this does not target diverse learning needs.

20. B: Before beginning fluency instruction, typically not before halfway through the first grade at the earliest, teachers should ensure that students have strong word recognition skills to provide the necessary foundation. Student speed and automaticity in decoding individual words are directly related to developing reading fluency (A): rapid, automatic word decoding is the precursor to fluent reading. Reading fluency not only indicates faster information processing, it also has a direct impact on comprehension (C) because the faster a student can process information, the better the student can comprehend what she reads. When a student must decode words more slowly and less automatically, both reading fluency and comprehension are decreased (D). Slow, conscious decoding does not increase comprehension by being more careful or thoughtful; instead, laborious student efforts to decode separate words for meaning divert the attention they could devote to overall comprehension if they could decode rapidly, effortlessly, and automatically.

21. C: Silent reading fluency can be monitored over time by giving the Test of Silent Contextual Reading Fluency (TSCRF) four times a year. A similar assessment tool is the Test of Silent Word Reading Fluency (TOSWRF), in which words of increasing complexity are given as a single, undifferentiated, and unpunctuated strand. As with the TSCRF, three minutes are given for the student to separate each word from the next. *Itwillcannotschoolbecomeagendaconsistentphilosophysuperfluous* is an example of such a strand.

22. B: Characters are always found in drama; they are also found in most fictional short stories and novels, and they are sometimes found in poems. Conflict (c) and action (d) are dramatic elements found not only in plays, but also frequently in short stories, novels, and poetry. Narrative (b) is typically found in novels and short stories; some poems also contain narratives (e.g., Longfellow's *The Song of Hiawatha*, Byron's *Childe Harold's Pilgrimage,* etc.). Although some plays include a narrator who periodically provides summaries, transitions, and/or commentaries, plays generally are LESS likely to contain narrative because the characters' actions tell the story.

23. D: Teachers can best employ strategic demands on children who are learning new vocabulary by beginning at a low level of demand and moving to high-demand questions. This effectively scaffolds new instruction by building up from simple and easy to complex and difficult. Alternation can be helpful as well, but instructing at a high level early on may result in confusion and frustration, rather than an improved grasp of a concept. (B) describes a constructivist approach to vocabulary, which can work for more abstract concepts. As students naturally encounter a concept, they build their own understanding of how something works. This approach may not be the best method for vocabulary acquisition, as students may arrive at inaccurate meanings. Similarly, (C) suggests keeping the rigor low until students have mastery over the new vocabulary, but vocabulary requires understanding terms in shallow and in deep ways and requires interaction with the word in a variety of applications to truly master a concept. Oversimplification can lead to inaccurate knowledge and possibly even frustration. Instead, a teacher should begin with a clear and simple definition and work toward complex applications as students are capable.

24. B: *Activating* is the term experts use to identify the reading strategy whereby the reader activates prior knowledge and applies it to the new information in reading to construct meaning from it. *Inferring* is a strategy whereby the reader combines what the text states explicitly with what it does not state but implies, and combines these both with what s/he already knows to draw inferences. *Questioning* is the reading strategy whereby the reader engages in "learning dialogues" with the text, author, classmates, and teachers to ask and answer questions about the text. *Summarizing* is the reading strategy whereby the reader paraphrases or restates what s/he perceives as the text's meaning.

25. A: Blogs (short for "web logs") are published online, where anybody with Internet access may read them. Bloggers may post occasionally, monthly, weekly, daily, or whenever they want. It is not uncommon for bloggers to post weekly or daily. Journals are more typical for private entries, similar to diaries. People often make journal entries daily or less often, similarly to blog posts but less publicly. (Some people also publish journals—in print or online as collections in books or e-books, or as ongoing online publications similar to blogs. However, journal writing is more often private, whereas blogging never is.) Letters are typically to others, not private (except for therapeutic letters written to vent emotions but never sent); and though sometimes published online (such as letters to the editor, open letters, or newsletters, among others), usually not daily. Essays are typically not written daily and privately or published online. Speeches are typically written for oral delivery, not daily online publication or as private activities.

26. C: Mnemonic devices help with remembering key sets of information by organizing it into patterns. For example, many mnemonic devices are made by identifying a series of initial letters corresponding to the words that must be remembered but forming an easily remembered acronym or phrase using the same initial letters (such as "RAFT" or "Role, Audience, Format, Topic" to help students remember the key elements of a writing assignment). The other answer choices reflect devices that are useful for reading and writing but are not specifically used for remembering key sets of information. Making outlines (A) helps with identifying main ideas and supporting details and organizing them into a hierarchy. Checklists (B) help ensure one has completed all steps or components of a task or project. Graphic organizers (D) help with visually representing abstract concepts and relationships.

27. D: The passage directly states that *Beowulf* is important because "it is often viewed as the first significant work of English literature," making D the correct answer choice.

28. A: The words in this question prompt are most often used to refer to *sounds* made while reading. Initial/onset, medial, and final sounds are decoded in the beginning, middle, and end of words. When a teacher needs to assess an emergent or struggling reader's ability to differentiate between sounds in words, he or she may use a phonological awareness assessment. This tool will provide the teacher with information about the student's current ability to decode or encode words.

29. C: Cross-cultural misunderstanding may occur when individuals are unaware of one another's perception of both verbal and nonverbal forms of communication. Such a situation during a family conference at school could limit the productivity and effectiveness of the meeting, offend the student's family, or discourage their further participation in the education program. Therefore, it is important that Ms. Benson is mindful of her use of verbal and nonverbal communication to ensure she is clear, professional, and respectful. Examples include body language, gestures, physical distance from the family, eye contact, and use of idioms when speaking.

30. A: Teachers should generally use a variety of formal and informal assessment instruments to get a complete picture of student achievement. This is especially applicable for grouping students, which teachers should never do for the long term based on the results of only one assessment instrument. To conduct formative assessments of learning in progress, teachers should use both formal and informal test instruments; and use several different kinds, rather than choosing only one formal instrument to use exclusively. Formative assessment results are valuable not only for evaluating student progress, but moreover for use in the classroom as teaching tools.

31. A: A soliloquy is a speech made by one character in a play speaking alone, as opposed to dialogue between/among multiple characters. Some poets (e.g., Robert Browning) have written entire poems in the voice of a single character; however, these are called dramatic monologues rather than soliloquies, a term generally reserved for drama, not poetry (B). Similarly, in novels (C), conversation between/among characters is called dialogue, whereas a long speech by one character would be called a monologue. Essays (D) are typically nonfiction and do not contain characters or their speech.

32. C: Point of view refers to the vantage point from which a story is written. First person uses the pronoun *I*. Second person uses the pronoun *you*. Third person uses the pronouns *he/she/they*. There is no fourth-person point of view. This passage was written in the third person.

33. D: The CALLA is a content-based approach to language instruction that integrates academic learning strategies that students require to participate in mainstream English-speaking classrooms. It includes objectives for content, language, and learning strategies, and it allows teachers to plan lessons using content based on themes or formats using sheltered content.

34. B: Metacognition refers to thinking about one's own thinking. Proficient readers use metacognitive skills to self-monitor their own understanding and make corrections when necessary. Making predictions, and then later assessing and revising them if necessary, demonstrates use of metacognitive skills. The other options require students to recall and/or analyze information, but they do not ask students to reflect on their own thinking.

35. B: Students high in the Bodily-Kinesthetic intelligence learn best through hands-on activities like dancing, sports, and using manipulatives. Those high in Intrapersonal intelligence excel at being in tune with, understanding, and explaining their own feelings; they learn best through reflective, metacognitive, and independent activities. Those high in the Naturalist intelligence type relate to the natural world and can identify and appreciate patterns in nature. They learn best by observing, studying, classifying, and collecting natural objects and/or studying or interacting with animals. Students high in the Visual-Spatial intelligence excel at visual perception and converting three-dimensional reality into two-dimensional media forms. They learn best through drawing, mapping, reading and making graphs and illustrations, and spatial visualization problems.

36. C: Once the students' notecards have been checked and edited for accuracy, they can easily be used to demonstrate the process of organizing ideas in an essay or research paper. Students can use their notecards as aids for making their outlines. They simply have to arrange the notecards in an appropriate order and add pertinent information to bridge the ideas together in their writing.

37. B: Jamie's teacher is teaching the class about many aspects of Mexican culture. It can be assumed that Jamie has prior knowledge of this topic, which comes in part from his family's past travels. While Jamie is engaged in the lesson, the verbal instruction and photographs "activate" or inspire recall of his prior knowledge of Spanish vocabulary. Jamie would not likely have been able to access this information without the visual and verbal cues, although it was still stored in his long-term memory.

38. B: For a variety of reasons, students' families may be hesitant to initiate communication with their children's school. This reticence could be due to work and lifestyle factors, previous negative encounters with the school system, or lack of confidence in their ability to become involved in their children's education in a meaningful way. By initiating and maintaining communication with students' families, the teacher establishes a welcoming environment in which families feel included as active participants in their children's education. As a result, family members feel encouraged and empowered to contribute to their children's learning both within and outside of the classroom, strengthening student development and achievement.

39. C: Summative assessments are administered after instruction and less often than formative assessments, which teachers make more frequently during instruction (A) to inform changes to make their teaching more effective (B). Typical times for summative assessments are after each lesson, unit, and school year is completed (C). Teachers rely on formative, not summative assessments for individual student data (D); they rely on summative assessment results for group data and group comparisons.

40. B: A KWL chart allows students to list they **K**now about a subject before they read, what they **W**ant to know or learn about it, and what they have **L**earned about it after reading. This is a good example of a research-based instructional strategy for activating students' prior knowledge. The teacher giving the students background information is the opposite of finding out what they already know. The teacher asking students what they know about the subject after they have read a text is also the opposite of the goal. Activating prior knowledge before reading enables students to build upon what they already know when they begin reading, as successful readers do, versus beginning to read without thinking, as less successful readers do. Similarly, the teacher should ask students their opinions and reactions about a topic before they read, not after, to activate their existing knowledge.

41. B: The verbs listed here all refer to taking pieces or parts of information or knowledge and bringing them together to create a whole, and to building relationships among the parts to fit new or different circumstances. Analysis is the opposite of synthesis—breaking information down into its component parts and demonstrating the relationships among those parts. An assignment for analysis would ask the student to compare, distinguish, test, categorize, examine, contrast, or analyze information. Evaluation is making judgments of information based on given criteria, confirming or supporting certain preferences, and persuading the reader. An assignment targeting evaluation would use words like evaluate, predict, appraise, conclude, score, judge, or compare. Application is using knowledge in new contexts. The assignment would ask the student to apply, prepare, practice, use, operate, sketch, calculate, solve, or illustrate.

42. A: Speakers can establish rapport and personal connection with audiences by making eye contact with the audience. Vocal tones (B) can be used to express enthusiasm, emphasize important points, and maintain audience attention, but it is not the most effective among these choices for building rapport. Articulation (C) is important for ensuring audience comprehension, but it is not as important as eye contact for building rapport. Similarly, body movement (D) is less crucial for rapport than eye contact is, though it is still important for emphasizing messages and maintaining the audience's attention.

43. B: A strong argument is not made by forcing people to pay attention, interrupting another speaker, or belittling an idea, person, or group. These behaviors simply weaken the speaker's position because they each demonstrate in a different way that the speaker is not in control of his own ideas, and must therefore try to control the situation by using emotion. The most successful arguments acknowledge the strongest points of the opposition, and then unemotionally dissect those points in order to find and demonstrate how they are flawed.

44. B: Research finds that the single greatest change in classroom instruction for improving student learning and achievement is feedback, which students and teachers get best from formative assessments. Summative assessments are best for comparison (A) of students to normative student samples, classes to statewide/nationwide classes at the same grade level, and schools to other schools, but they do not give such immediate feedback during ongoing instruction (C). Although they yield more individual student data, formative assessments are typically informal and not standardized and hence are not used to make comparisons (D) the way that standardized summative assessments are.

45. C: Conrad's novel deals with characters in colonial Africa, so post-colonial theories would most inform considering how the author treats those characters. Aristotle's theory of unity would be more likely to inform *Oedipus Rex* by Sophocles, Homer's *Iliad* and *Odyssey*, and many other similar—especially classical—works meeting Aristotle's criteria for unity of plot. Feminist and gender theories are more likely to inform a work like *The Awakening* (1899) by Kate Chopin and have popularly been applied to Shakespeare's *The Taming of the Shrew*; Hardy's *Tess of the D'Urbervilles;* D.H. Lawrence's *Women in Love;* and the works of Jane Austen, George Eliot, Charlotte Brontë, and Virginia Woolf, among many others. Marxist theories are more likely to inform the interactions of characters according to their historical and cultural background, social class, and economic circumstances. For example, some have applied Marxist criticism to Ferrol Sams' novel *Run with the Horsemen* (1982) or Langston Hughes' poem "Union" (Collected Poems, 1921-1940).

46. D: Research-based vocabulary instruction findings show that children need ample word repetition, but not through drilling. Multiple exposures to the same words in different contexts are more effective. Multiple and repeated exposures are important because children do not learn vocabulary through only one or two exposures to a new word. Research finds that they do not simply learn vocabulary in texts indirectly from reading; instead, teachers must give them direct instruction in the new vocabulary words they find in their texts.

47. C: Before Charles Darwin published *On the Origin of Species* (1859), Carl Linnaeus (1735) and John Ray's (1686-1691) work showed resistance to ideas of evolution, so choice C is correct. Their work reflected the Royal Society's post-English Civil War (1642-1651) reaction—both against science threatening stability and in favor of scientific work that would maintain it. Choice A is incorrect because Georges Buffon suggested (1766) some similar-looking animal species could share common ancestries, supporting ideas of evolution. Choice B is incorrect because Georges Cuvier's paleontology research supported the idea of evolution by finding fossils of past species resembling modern animal versions (1799), proving extinction and supporting functional adaptation. Choice D is incorrect because Jean-Baptiste Lamarck's theory (1809) that living things adapted to environments, inherited adaptations, and developed increasing complexity supported Darwin's ideas.

48. D: Part of building literacy skills is showing students how to listen effectively to various types of texts: narrative, poetry, informative, etc. In order to become competent in a variety of literacy skills, students must be able to listen for information and for pleasure/experience. This teacher is not only exposing them to poetry, but creating a forum in which they can actively listen and then discuss what they have experienced or learned. The scenario given in Choice A could possibly be true, as could Choice C. But it is less likely that the teacher would devote an entire month of reading and listening to a specific type of text simply to give her students a break or to make a point about poetry versus prose. Choice B assumes that the poetry she reads will rhyme, which is not always the case.

49. A: The focus of this activity is on comparing the meanings of the words before and after the suffix *less* is added. Students should recognize that the newly formed words mean *without* (base word) and be able to apply this knowledge to figure out the meanings of other words containing the same suffix. While students may also learn to spell and decode words containing *less* as a result of this activity, the primary focus is on the words' meanings. Choice D is incorrect because *less* is a suffix. Prefixes are letters or groups of letters added to the beginnings of words.

50. A: Although the popular modern definition of comedy equates it with humor and making people laugh, this was NOT the ancient Greeks' Classical definition, to which Shakespeare and others also adhered, that comedy may or may not be funny, but it always has a happy ending (b). Ancient

Greek, Elizabethan and Renaissance, and modern definitions of tragedy all include sad endings, often involving death (c). According to Aristotle, tragedy should evoke audience emotional responses of terror and pity (d) to be effective.

51. B: While the school is making an appropriate exception for religious accommodations, which is legally and ethically appropriate, maintaining a policy that prohibits other headwear could unintentionally highlight differences and embarrass the student instead of normalizing her dress. The school staff has not done anything wrong in this scenario, but they may want to consider expanding the dress code to allow for a broader application of cultural variation in dress.

52. C: Using context clues can help the reader determine the meanings of many unknown words quickly and also contribute to reading comprehension. Asking a classmate for the meanings of words may work in the short term, but it does not help the reader develop independent reading strategies, and there may not always be another person present while reading. Looking up the unknown words later may result in the student missing words that are critical to the meaning of the text, negatively affecting comprehension. Similarly, while skipping over the unknown words may result in sentences that appear to make sense, the missing words may play important roles in the meaning.

53. A: One research-based writing instruction strategy teachers can use is to give students explicit instruction in combining simple sentences into compound, complex, and compound-complex sentences. This develops student ability to compose more sophisticated sentences. Computer word-processing programs are not crutches and do not interfere with independent student writing skills; on the contrary, teachers can use these as a strategy to help students engage in the processes of planning, writing, and editing more easily. A process writing approach is another research-based instructional strategy, not an incompatible one. It allows students extended practice with planning, composing, and reviewing; interacting with classmates while writing; owning writing responsibility; writing for real audiences; and self-evaluating writing. Research finds that teachers should not only provide good models of writing types and help them analyze these, but also encourage them to emulate these models in their own writing efforts.

54. B: In a cloze test, a reader is given a text with certain words blocked out. The reader must be able to determine probable missing words based on contextual clues. In order to supply these words, the reader must already know them.

55. B: Relational messages, as opposed to content messages, are concerned with the relationship between a speaker and a recipient rather than with the overt subject of the communication. They may convey belonging, respect, or disapproval, among other things. They are frequently largely or entirely nonverbal; because of this, they may be supported with verbal feedback to confirm them. The content of the message, "Should I come over after work?" is a logistical request. If a speaker leans forward to touch a recipient who is weeping, the relational message is "Do you need my support?" The recipient might respond with a nod and a grateful look, or might clarify the speaker's offer by saying, "I won't be good company, but you can come."

56. D: Of the choices, this is the best activity for developing critical listening skills to evaluate message credibility. Option (A) best develops vocabulary and comprehension as well as spoken language enjoyment: until around 8th grade, children's listening levels far exceed their reading levels, so hearing books above reading level expands language development. Five- and 6-year-olds commonly understand and enjoy this book written on a 4th-grade reading level. While it is not too early to introduce critical thinking questions (e.g., "What do you think will happen next?", "What would you do in this situation?" etc.), K-1 students *more* likely appreciate and enjoy spoken language. Listening to *The Bells* (B) would require some basic analytical skills of 6th-graders for recognizing the obvious effects of Poe's use of heavy repetition, rhyme, alliteration, onomatopoeia, etc. However, they would likely respond more by appreciating and enjoying the evocative sounds of the language. Most students enjoy nonsense words (D) and Carroll's creativity and humor in *Jabberwocky* (from *Through the Looking-Glass*) more than critically evaluating the poem.

57. C: Literacy skills are various and include a number of different sub-skills: reading fluency, comprehension, application of knowledge, listening, speaking, grammar, spelling, writing, and more. It is important for teachers to track student development for lesson design and to communicate with the student, future teachers, and parents. Therefore, it is best to keep samples of a variety of assessments, including descriptions of reading fluency, writing samples, projects, and formal assessments of grammar, spelling, and other skills. All of these skills develop simultaneously, but at different rates. Therefore, it is impossible to judge a student's literacy based only on one measure of assessment.

58. C: There is currently a wide variety of technology resources available that can support class instruction. However, teachers must choose carefully in order to ensure that the technology is useful and relevant to the intended learning outcomes for the class. The language lab described allows students to experience text through both listening and reading, thereby utilizing different processes in the brain. The interactive modules also support decoding and comprehension skills that go along with the texts. This use of technology reinforces important skills in a way that will be unique and interesting for the students.

59. D: Teachers will observe a variety of developmental arcs when teaching reading, since all students learn differently. It is very important to understand which instances are normal in the course of learning and which signal a learning difficulty. Barrett is still exhibiting confusion over certain letter-sounds, typically when the letters look similar. At his age, this difficulty could suggest that Barrett has an issue with reading that could be addressed by a reading specialist. The other three choices describe normal behaviors that are commonly exhibited by children when they are learning to read. Choice C, Noelle, may describe an instance in which a student is having a learning problem. However, the teacher will need more information about Noelle's reading skills besides her reluctance to read before making a determination about how to proceed.

60. D: According to research-based writing instruction strategies, when teachers assign students to small collaborative writing groups, they should set individual performance expectations for within-group as well as individual work. Teachers should also support student groups by providing them with structure. Classmates in collaborative writing groups should give each other both positive feedback for reinforcement and constructive feedback for correction as well.

61. D: A bildungsroman is a term for a novel in which the main character comes of age, develops, learns, and/or grows; an elegy is a term for a poem which mourns the dead. Picaresque refers to a novel about the misadventures of a roguish protagonist; epistolary refers to a novel written in the form of letters/telegrams/other correspondence (A). Fictional novels can be historical, i.e., based on actual events and characters in history, or speculative, i.e., exploring not actual/current/historical but potential/future events/developments (B). Nonfictional essays can be persuasive, i.e., aiming to convince readers of a position, or expository, i.e., aiming to impart information (C).

62. D: Collaborative Strategic Reading (CSR) is a technique that largely depends on cooperative learning and practice of metacognition. In practice, this look slike putting students into groups and having them self-monitor their own reading comprehension using various reading strategies. One popular reading strategy that can be used includes "click and clunk," which is where students report which parts of the story *click* to them, or which makes sense without much difficulty, and which parts *clunk*, or are not easy to understand. Then the group would collaborate to resolve the clunks and ensure everyone understood the reading assignment. Other strategies can include use of context clues, rereading, or any other reading comprehension strategy, paired with group discussion.

63. B: This is an example of a closed question because the student can only answer "simile" or "metaphor" without needing to elaborate unless asked to explain the answer. In contrast, choice C is an open-ended question because the student must both define simile and metaphor and explain the difference between them. Choice A is an open-ended literature question because the student cannot answer with yes, no, or some other single word or short phrase; he or she has to describe the action or events in a story that represent its climax, which requires understanding story structure, story elements, knowing the definition of a story's climax, reading the story, and understanding it. Choice D is a very open-ended question, as students have considerable latitude in giving the reasons each of them perceives for having poetry.

64. C: A stanza consists of a grouping of lines, set off by a space, that usually has a set pattern of meter and rhyme. This poem has six stanzas.

65. A: The previous stanza gives clues as to whom *we* refers:

> "Not one would mind, neither bird nor tree
> If mankind perished utterly"

We is referencing mankind.

66. A: Both similes and metaphors make comparisons, but not in the same way. A simile uses words such as like or as, while a metaphor discards these words, usually referring to one thing as another to show what they have in common, such as referring to a crowd as "a sea of faces" to show how large it is.

67. B: In the Spanish language, the letter h is typically silent. Because the student is an ELL and the USA has many people—both immigrants and those born here—whose first and/or only language is Spanish, this is the first factor to consider among the choices. An articulation disorder (A) is possible, but the teacher should not assume this first with an ELL student. (An SLP evaluation can determine the difference.) While a hearing assessment (C) is always a good idea, if /h/ omission were due to hearing loss the student would likely omit or distort other unvoiced fricatives like /f/, /s/, /ʃ/, and /θ/. If the student had a breathing problem (D), other symptoms would occur in addition to not articulating /h/.

68. C: Except in the case of very brief texts, every writer will need to transition from one idea to another. If not done correctly, the abrupt switch from one topic to another will be jarring to the reader. This can be avoided by using transitional paragraphs to smoothly move the text from one topic to another.

69. A: The text at hand contains several clues as to the meaning of this word, including the use of the words "peaceful" and "quiet" in the preceding sentence. Students may also recognize that Mom's requests for help with undesirable household chores interrupted Dad's peaceful, quiet 'reverie." Choice A is the specific method that would be most appropriate for determining the word's meaning; Choice B is a less reliable or systematic way of doing the same thing. Choice C would not be helpful in this case since "reverie" is not a word that can be decoded in a traditional manner.

Choice D would not offer a realistic solution to this question since previewing and reviewing are more helpful in increasing comprehension of informative texts, rather than vocabulary words.

70. A: Asking students to create lists of what skills they feel they are strong in allows the teacher to informally assess what students know as well as learn about the students' interests. This should allow the teacher to use their strengths and interests to better plan instruction and activities in the classroom. Asking students to create a list of strengths is not a formal assessment and should not be used as an all-inclusive tool to assess the background knowledge of a student. While the teacher may be able to use the list of tasks as a way of gauging what students know, self-reported strengths on the first day of school are insufficient to make grouping decisions. Although creating a list of tasks that students can perform may increase student confidence temporarily, it is not the ultimate purpose of this activity and is instead a secondary benefit.

71. C: Oral language is a vital aspect of any language arts instruction. Often, the first concepts of language are transmitted via oral and auditory processes. The first Americans also possessed a rich oral culture in which stories and histories were passed down through generations via storytelling. Inviting a guest speaker who is part of this culture helps students understand more about cultures in their world, as well as the value of oral language and storytelling. This introduction gives students a relevant personal experience with which to connect what they will be learning in class.

72. D: Teachers should give students learning English as a second language (ESL) and English language learners (ELLs) clear models and examples of what they expect them to do, how to do it, and how the completed results should look. Stating directions verbally in English alone is insufficient for students learning a foreign language. Teachers must also give ELLs more time to respond because it takes them longer to process the English they hear, mentally translate it into their own language, mentally formulate a response in their own language, translate that mentally into English, and judge whether their translation makes sense before they answer. It typically takes ESLs years before they can "think in English." When using idioms and figures of speech, teachers should explain these to ELLs and add pantomime demonstrations to help them understand. These expressions are not logical and often have no L1 equivalents for ESLs, so they require explicit instruction.

73. B: Authors of informational texts may occasionally explicitly state their point of view, but there are more cases where the author is acting as an expert, a neutral observer, or some other ostensibly objective voice. Therefore, readers will often need to infer the author's point of view. Choice A is incorrect because there is no requirement in informational writing that the author's point of view be part of the main idea. Choice C is incorrect because seeing the author's point of view is generally easier when the author is extreme or opinionated and harder when they seem neutral or balanced. This also means that some analysis is usually required, but the need for analysis does not indicate that the writing is poor, so choice D is incorrect.

74. A: Introducing new vocabulary words will help students decode the words faster when they are encountered in the text, thus assisting with fluency. Recognizing the words and knowing their meanings will also build readers' confidence. Additionally, explaining the meanings of the words in advance will help students comprehend the text when they read it independently. Reading the first few pages aloud without discussion will not help students recognize or understand the vocabulary words, nor will it highlight important words beyond the first few pages. Listing what students want to learn about the topic helps to set a purpose for reading, not explain vocabulary. Predicting helps students activate prior knowledge, make connections, and stay actively engaged in the reading process.

75. B: Early Production, with the characteristics named, is the second stage of ESL acquisition. Preproduction (A), the first stage, involves no English speech, minimal listening comprehension, and the ability to draw pictures of and/or point at objects represented by some English words. Speech Emergence (C) is the third stage, characterized by good English comprehension; English speech using simple sentences, but still showing pronunciation and grammatical errors; and frequently misunderstanding English-language jokes. Intermediate Fluency (D), the fourth stage, features excellent English listening comprehension and few spoken grammatical errors.

76. C: Many factors can affect a student's ability to understand what he or she is reading. Building comprehension skills is an ongoing process and can be made difficult if a student lacks the appropriate level of reading fluency. If he or she cannot read accurately or with enough speed, he or she will have much more trouble with comprehension than the average student. It is important to identify any decoding or vocabulary problems that might be affecting comprehension first; if those can be solved, comprehension skills may naturally increase as reading fluency increases.

77. B: Bottom-up listening strategies are text-based: listeners ascertain meaning from the language used in the text by listening to identify specific details, syntactic patterns, cognates, etc. Top-down listening strategies are listener-based: listeners activate their own background knowledge of the subject matter, context, situation, text genre or type, and language used to ascertain the main idea (A) in the text; to be able to summarize its content (C); and to interpret text by making inferences and predicting (D) what may come next.

78. B: Early ballad themes included jealousy, betrayal, murder, war, famine, poverty, etc. as well as love; early sonnet themes included politics, social standing, satire, etc. as well as love. Both genres have prominently featured expressions of love. The sonnet has five main kinds (A): the Petrarchan/Italian, Occitan, Shakespearean/English, Spenserian, and Modern; the ballad has developed many more variations in form. Originally the ballad was often set to music, and it was later associated with operas and musicals; the sonnet originated in dramatic plays and medieval courts. Though some sonnets have been set to music, the sonnet did not originate with music (C). The standard ballad meter is iambic heptameter, albeit with variations; the standard sonnet meter is iambic pentameter (D).

79. B: Because they are done during learning in progress, formative assessments enable teachers to make changes to their instruction via the feedback the assessment gives them. If one strategy or technique is not working, they can modify it or substitute another one, increase or decrease the pace of procedures, increase or decrease repetitions, or change instructional modalities (among others) to tailor instruction to the individual student's learning rates, needs, styles, preferences, and interests to optimize learning. Hence formative assessments also help students meet standards-based goals on time. Summative assessments cannot do this because they are given after instruction is completed and less often, so they do not allow time to change ongoing instruction to expedite progress. Formative assessments typically involve students more in the assessment processes, not summative assessments. Summative assessments are more often used to provide accountability and to calculate student grades, not formative assessments.

80. A: Technical passages focus on presenting specific information and have a tone of formality. They also usually prompt a response from their recipient. Expository passages reveal information to the reader. This passage does give information, but the information is specific, technical, and meant to prompt action from the students receiving the email. Therefore, technical (A) is the best answer. Narrative writing focuses on telling a story, and the passage offers no indication of this. Persuasive writing attempts to persuade the reader to agree with a certain position; the instructor offers the students information and advice but leaves the decision up to each student.

81. C: Factors that can often prevent diverse parents and families from communicating and participating in the education of their children include language barriers, which frequently stop them from communicating (A); unsuccessful parent school histories, which can make them feel ineffectual to participate (B); feeling alienated from school processes because of their differing cultures (C) and/or languages; and poor past experiences with schools, which can make them reluctant to participate (D).

82. D: Virginia Woolf had a powerful effect on the modern novel. Other authors that influenced the Modernist movement include T. S. Eliot, Ezra Pound, James Joyce, and Gertrude Stein. The Modernist movement took place in the late 19th and early 20th centuries. The authors questioned traditional forms of literature and in doing so, wrote novels and poems that were full of modern thought.

83. D: Teachers should try to avoid shallow notions of what it means to provide cultural or multi-cultural education; in Choice "a", we cannot presume to understand another person by listening to his favorite music or watching a favorite movie. In Choice "b", there is also the assumption that there is a variety of musical tastes in the class, which may not be the case. In fact, if many students pick the same song, it is possible to use that choice to open up dialogue about what they lyrics mean and why they are so popular with the class. Choice "c" is posed in direct opposition to Choice "d". However, Choice "d" suggests what most teachers know to be true: literacy skills are not just important for schoolwork and class work; students must be able to take meaning from a variety of different sources in order to grow into educated adults. Music is an important medium through which students can express themselves and learn about the world around them through comprehension and listening skills.

84. D: Unlike individualistic American culture, some collectivist cultures prohibit displaying wealth through dressing expensively. Similarly, teachers cannot assume parents reticent about their own education lack it (C); they may conceal it out of modesty. Cultural and religious rules vary widely across cultures; head-patting or hair-ruffling with young children, considered harmless in America, is alarming or prohibited in other countries (B). Facial expressions like smiles are universally understandable, but personal distance from others during interactions varies widely across cultures (A).

85. C: She should locate the vowels, then locate familiar word parts. Syllables are organized around vowels. In order to determine the syllables, this student should begin by locating the vowels. It's possible to have a syllable that is a single vowel *(a/gain)*. It isn't possible to have a syllable that is a single consonant. Once the word has been broken into its component syllables the reader is able to study the syllables to find ones that are familiar and might give her a clue as to the word's meaning, such as certain prefixes or suffixes.

86. B: The division described in the question is termed a *stanza* in poetry. A verse (A) is a single line rather than a group of lines, as far as poetry is concerned—though in songs it is a group of lines, like a stanza in a poem. A refrain (C) is a verse, set of verses, or set of words that is repeated regularly throughout a ballad, other poem, or song. A paragraph (D) is like a stanza in that it expresses a group of related ideas and it is separate from other paragraphs. However, it is used in prose, not in poetry.

87. A: This sentence is an analogy, which compares two concepts to establish a relationship, so choice A is correct. Analogy can enhance comprehension of a new concept via comparison to an older or more familiar concept. Allegory (B) uses symbolism to represent an abstract concept with a more concrete concept. Allusion (C) is a passing reference to a specific work, place, person, or event. For example, saying "Susan loves to help and care for other people so much that her friends call her Mother Teresa" is an allusion to a famous person that makes a point about how compassionate someone is. Antithesis (D) juxtaposes words, phrases, or sentences with opposite meanings, balancing these to add insight. A good example is Neil Armstrong's statement during the moon landing: "That's one small step for man, one giant leap for mankind."

88. B: Typical speech is roughly 125 words per minute, while typical thinking is estimated at roughly 500 words per minute. This natural disparity does not make listening less effective than reading. While the slower rate of speech and the faster rate of thought does allow students' minds to wander, teachers can have students make use of this time by instructing them to summarize mentally the speech they hear as an active listening technique. This enables students to process, consider, and manipulate heard information and make richer, more creative decisions about it. Listening and learning share the common characteristics of being both social and reciprocal.

89. A: In (A), the teacher guides previewing of information to show students how to put themselves in the right frame of mind to listen carefully for meaning. Students are then able to listen in a guided way based upon the previewing. By varying the type of comprehension assessment, the teacher will get a better understanding of what the students learned. (B) is a good exercise but does not provide for direct instruction by the teacher or a particularly skilled student. In (C), students are focusing more on reading comprehension than listening since they must read the story to themselves and then write a report. There is then no way to gauge what they have learned. (D) would be useful but does not include teacher-guided previewing, which is very helpful in building comprehension.

90. B: As the students strive to understand individuals from around the world, the project would not be complete without attention to that individual's mode of oral expression. In reading about and repeating the research subject's own words, the students will have an opportunity, if guided appropriately, to learn about how a person's speech reflects their identity and thoughts. The students will assume the role of a person very different from themselves and be able to place themselves into another perspective via oral language.